POCKET GUIDE

TREES

OF ZAMBIA

Adam

DEDICATION

Published by Struik Nature
(an imprint of Penguin Random House
South Africa (Pty) Ltd)
Reg. No. 1953/000441/07

The Estuaries No. 4, Oxbow Crescent,
Century Avenue, Century City, 7441
PO Box 1144, Cape Town, 8000
South Africa

First published in 2023

10 9 8 7 6 5 4 3 2 1

Publisher: Pippa Parker
Managing editor: Roelien Theron
Editor: Natalie Bell
Designer & cartographer: Gillian Black
Concept design: Janice Evans
Proofreader: Emsie du Plessis
Picture research: Colette Stott

Reproduction by Studio Repro
Printed and bound in China by
Golden Prosperity Printing & Packaging
(Heyuan) Co., Ltd.

MIX
Paper from responsible sources
FSC® C146541
www.fsc.org

Visit **struiknature.co.za** and join the Struik Nature Club for updates, news, events and special offers.

Cover: *Adansonia digitata;* **Back cover, top to bottom:** *Markhamia obtusifolia, Borassus aethiopium, Ximenia caffra, Diospyros mespiliformis, Breonadia salicina;* **Title page:** Palms, Maramba River; **Opposite:** *Syzygium guineense,* Kafue River

ISBN 978 1 77584 845 5 (Print)
ISBN 978 1 77584 846 2 (ePub)

Although this book draws on a large number of botanical sources, any errors, omissions or misconceptions are entirely our own, and for this reason we welcome feedback. We hope that this book will encourage contributions to the Flora of Zambia website.

CONTENTS

EXPLORING ZAMBIA'S TREES

Zambia is a large landlocked country in central southern Africa, characterised by a variety of different terrains and a rich diversity of plant and wildlife. Around 863 tree species are found here, 41 of which are globally threatened. This pocket guide describes 140 tree species commonly seen in Zambia, with a handful of spectacular trees and four naturalised exotics.

Zambia's wildlife-protected areas cover almost a third of the country. The 20 national parks offer some of the best tree viewing in natural environments. These national parks are clearly marked on the map on page 5.

In the past decades, tree cover in Zambia has significantly reduced owing to the effects of global warming, increasing droughts and the ongoing clearing of forests. But a growing awareness of the value of trees, not least to mitigate climate change, has led to an increased commitment to conserve local forest reserves and woodlands. It is our hope that this book will inspire improved protection of Zambia's wonderful indigenous trees through an understanding of their importance in our environment.

Vital ecological associations

All trees benefit from the ecological services provided by a host of life forms.

Trees and termitaria

Termite mounds are a common sight in Zambia's landscapes, often with trees growing directly on them or close by. These massive columns are in fact cooling towers constructed by colonies of subterranean termites. The worked soil, turned and pushed from underground, brings nutrients and moisture to plant root systems and the soil's surface. From above, rainwater percolates easily through the loosened soil, also moving organic matter – not least carbon – back into the lower horizons. Passing birds perch on termite mounds and scatter seeds in their droppings or while eating. The nutrient-rich termite mound soil offers ideal germination conditions for these seeds, and it is not unusual for large termitaria to host numerous plant species.

Typical termite mound–plant association

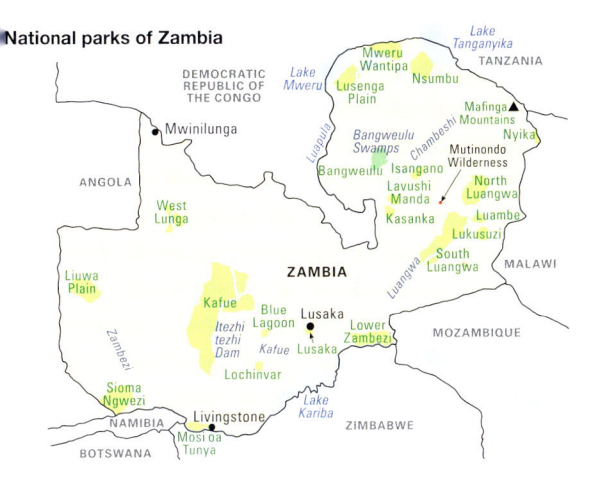

National parks of Zambia

Pollinators

Insect pollinators, particularly bees, moths and wasps, perform a vital service for trees. As they go about their daily lives, visiting floral food sources, they ensure that new generations of trees can germinate from the resulting fruit and seeds. Where pollination is not by wind or other transfer mechanisms, pollinators ensure that male pollen is moved to female stigmas, thus fertilising the flowers' ovaries.

Bees pollinating *Oncoba spinosa*

Trunk of bee tree with hive of wild bees

Fungi

Some fungi are known to form complex relationships with the roots of trees. The mycelium – the underground branching part of a fungus that functions much like a plant's root system – is made up fine filaments, called hyphae, that create an elaborate network linking the roots of trees growing near another. The hyphae permit the exchange of nutrients, sugars and water between the tree and the fungus. Edible fungi are a valuable human and animal food source when the fruiting bodies emerge as mushrooms during the rainy season.

Giant mushroom, Kasanka National Park, Serenje

Zambezi escarpment vegetation above Lake Kariba

VEGETATION TYPES AND TREE DISTRIBUTION

There are 11 major vegetation types in Zambia, reflecting the geological and ecological transitions across the country. The most extensive types are dry evergreen forest, Miombo and Munga woodland, and dry *Baikiaea* forest. Others are more localised and some are patchy and too small to show on the vegetation map below. The distribution of vegetation types reflects annual rainfall, ranging from around 1,500mm in the north to 600mm in the south and the west, and in low-altitude valleys. Vegetation is also influenced by the geological and soil conditions in a region. Soils on the weathered plateau in the north and centre are acidic, while those associated with Zambia's major river systems are fertile alluvial soils. The southwest is covered in deep Kalahari Sand. Each vegetation type comprises a variety of tree and other plant species.

Major vegetation types of Zambia

1 Dry evergreen *Marquesia–Parinari* forest
2 Dry evergreen *Cryptosepalum* forest
3 Montane forest
4 Dry deciduous Itigi forest
5 Dry deciduous *Baikiaea* forest
6 Miombo woodland
7 Kalahari woodland
8 Munga woodland (savanna)
9 Zambezian and Mopane woodlands
10 Western Kalahari grassland
11 Floodplain grassland
Lakes
Major rivers

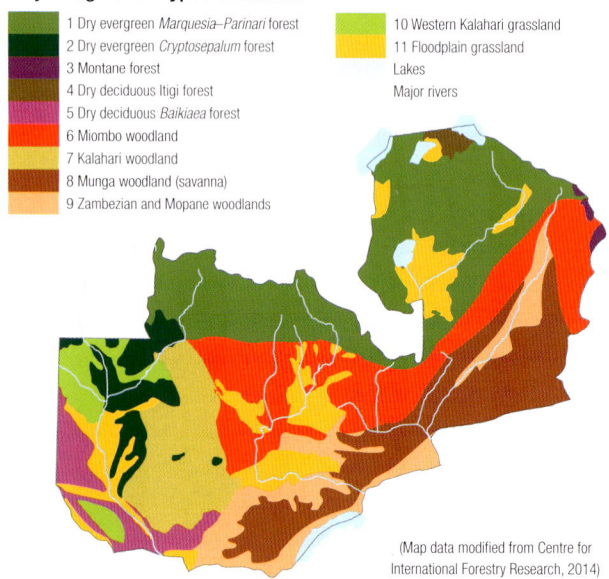

(Map data modified from Centre for International Forestry Research, 2014)

Forest

1 Dry evergreen *Marquesia–Parinari* forest: Dominated by high-canopy, buttressed forms of *Marquesia* and *Parinari*, this forest is confined to northern and western Zambia's high-rainfall area (receiving over 1,100mm per year). It has three layers: a closed canopy reaching about 25m, a patchy middle storey of 10–15m, and shrubs, scramblers and herbs at ground level, with much open ground.

Marquesia forest

2 Dry evergreen *Cryptosepalum* forest: Occurring in the western Kalahari basin, this forest comprises three storeys: *Cryptosepalum* and *Baikiaea* species in the canopy, a thicket-shrub storey locally called 'mavunda', and an extensive mossy and herb ground cover.

Extensive *Cryptosepalum* forest

3 Wet forest and montane forest: Three types of wet forest are confined to high-altitude, high-rainfall areas in the northeast, north and northwest of Zambia: montane, swamp and riparian. Occurring only on the northeastern Nyika Plateau and the Mafinga Mountains, montane forest comprises three storeys, with the canopy dominated by *Pouteria*, *Podocarpus* and *Parinari* species.

Montane forest and wetland

Swamp and riparian wet forests: These forests occupy localised areas along major rivers and streams, mainly in the wetter northern region. (Distributions too small to show on the map.)

4 Dry deciduous Itigi forest: Confined to the northern depression between Lake Mweru-wa-Ntipa and Lake Tanganyika, Itigi is a deciduous two-storey forest with a low canopy dominated by *Baphia*, *Boscia*, *Bussea* and *Diospyros* species and *Euphorbia candelabrum*. The understorey comprises diverse thicket with little grass.

Dry deciduous Itigi forest

5 Dry deciduous *Baikiaea* forest: Found on well-drained Kalahari Sand in western and southwestern Zambia, *Baikiaea* forest has two storeys. The canopy is dominated by the extremely fire-sensitive and heavily logged red hardwoods, *Baikiaea plurijuga* and *Pterocarpus antunesii*. The understorey comprises deciduous scrambling shrubs and herbs supplemented during the rainy months by a proliferation of herbs and grasses.

Woodland

Chipya woodland: This occurs in patches next to dry evergreen forest around the Bangweulu basin. Considered to be a form of dry evergreen forest that has been degraded by fire, this wooded grassland comprises three storeys: a diverse evergreen and deciduous canopy at about 20m, a shrub storey and understoreys, and prolific ground flora of herbs and tall grasses. Chipya includes species of *Parinari*, *Erythrophleum*, *Ficus*, *Afzelia*, *Acacia*, *Albizia* and *Terminalia*. (Distributions too small to show on the map.)

6 Miombo woodland: The most extensive vegetation type, covering about 45 per cent of Zambia, this two-storey (reaching 15–21m) open-canopy woodland is dominated by *Brachystegia*, *Julbernardia* and *Isoberlinia* species, from the legume family (Fabaceae). In the wetter north, *Marquesia macroura* is also common. The lower storey varies with soil and rainfall conditions. (Almost all Miombo woodland is now considered to be secondary growth following clearing, cultivation and/or severe burning over the last two centuries.)

7 Kalahari woodland: Found predominantly on Kalahari Sand in western and northwestern Zambia, but with outliers in the lower Kafue, lower Zambezi and Luangwa valleys, Kalahari woodland is a two-storey, semi-deciduous vegetation type. Dominant canopy species vary with location and include members of *Guibourtia*, *Burkea*, *Diplorhynchus*, *Parinari*, *Erythrophleum*, *Pterocarpus*, *Combretum*, *Terminalia* and *Ricinodendron*. *Brachystegia spiciformis* and *B. longifolia* are invading this woodland.

Dry deciduous *Baikiaea* forest

Chipya woodland

Miombo woodland

Kalahari woodland

8 Munga woodland (savanna): Occurring mostly on sandy clay soils along the edges of valley systems, mainly in central, eastern and southern Zambia, this two-storey woodland is species-diverse, deciduous, open and park-like, with a patchy understorey. Dominant trees in the canopy are species of *Acacia*, *Terminalia* and *Combretum*, but numerous other genera are common, including *Adonsonia*, *Afzelia*, *Burkea*, *Diplorhynchus*, *Erythrophleum*, *Kigelia*, *Peltophorum*, *Pericopsis*, *Piliostigma*, *Pseudolachnostylis*, *Pterocarpus* and the palms *Hyphaene* and *Borassus*. Sometimes thickets form, with *Commiphora*, *Markhamia* and *Euphorbia* species being common.

Munga woodland

9a Zambezian woodland (combined with Mopane woodland on map): Occurring on both Kalahari and alluvial sands in the lower Kafue, lower Zambezi and Luangwa valleys, Zambezian woodland is a two-storey, semi-deciduous variant of Kalahari woodland. Canopy dominants vary with location and soil type, but may include *Burkea*, *Combretum*, *Diplorhynchus*, *Erythrophleum*, *Faidherbia*, *Parinari*, *Pterocarpus*, *Schinziophyton* and *Terminalia*.

Zambezian woodland – *Faidherbia* stand

9b Mopane woodland (combined with Zambezian woodland on map): Mopane woodland has vigorously invaded non-flooded alluvial zones in all the major low-altitude, low-rainfall valleys, often on saline, alkali-rich sandy clays. It is an open, single-storey deciduous woodland, usually with almost pure stands of *Colophospermum mopane*. Other genera may include Munga or Kalahari species: *Acacia*, *Adansonia*, *Albizia*, *Balanites*, *Baphia*, *Combretum*, *Kirkia*, *Lannea*, *Philenoptera*, *Pterocarpus* and *Sclerocarya*.

Mopane woodland

Typical upper floodplain grassland

Grassland

All of Zambia's major grasslands are partly or completely flooded in the wet season and dry in the winter months.

10 Western Kalahari grassland:
Occurring on Kalahari Sand in western Zambia, usually above the high flood level, it is characterised by the grass genera *Hyparrhenia*, *Echinochloa* and *Vossia* (where wetter), with occasional trees or tree clumps comprising *Acacia*, *Burkea*, *Diplorhynchus* and *Guibourtia* species, and *Parinari capensis* – a suffrutex (often extensive).

Western Kalahari grassland

11 Floodplain grassland:
Seasonal grasslands occur on Kalahari Sand in the west, and on alluvial soils, most extensively in the Kafue and Chambeshi valleys, offering rich, early dry-season grazing. Typical grasses are species of *Echinochloa*, *Leersia* and *Panicum*.

Floodplain grassland

Dambo grassland: Localised at the head of streams, these grasslands occur in the wetter central and northern river catchments. Species vary from members of *Hyparrhenia* and other coarse grasses on the periphery, to sedges (*Eleocharis*, *Scirpus*) in the centre and outflow. (Distributions too small to show on the map.)

Backswamp grassland: These seasonal grasslands, along major rivers subject to overbank flooding, comprise *Loudetia*, *Echinochloa* and *Eragrostis* species and *Cyperus papyrus* (papyrus) and *Phragmites* reed beds in swampy areas. (Distributions too small to show on the map.)

GUIDE TO THE SPECIES ACCOUNTS

The species in this book have been divided into five groups.

Group 1   **Palms**
Group 2   **Exuding sap** or **latex** when damaged (with various leaf forms)
Group 3   **Simple** and **mainly opposite** or **whorled** leaf arrangements
Group 4   **Simple** and **mainly alternate** leaf arrangements
Group 5   **Compound** leaves:

  - 2 or 3 leaflets in various arrangements
  - pinnate with a **single terminal leaflet** (imparipinnate)
  - pinnate with **paired terminal leaflets** (paripinnate)
  - bipinnate with **twice-compound leaves** that have leaflets along the secondary veins

Page 12 lists plant families and genera, together with typical characteristics.

1 **Leaf type** for species

2 **Local names** are given, following this sequence: Bemba, Kunda, Kaonde, Lozi, Lenje, Lunda, Nyanja, Soli, Tonga, Tumbuka. Only the most widely used names are listed.

3 **subsp.** = subspecies; **var.** = variety – given in first line of account

4 **H** = height (mostly maximum tree height is given); **S** = spread (width) of crown

5 **Distinctive features**

6 **Distribution map**

7 **Other species** lists others in the genus occurring in Zambia, and mentions similar-looking species where identities could be confused.

8 **Colour-coded footers** feature common and family names.

Acacia polyacantha   White Thorn

LOCAL NAMES: Mungansussi, Chibombo, Mukotokoto, Chombwe, Ngowe, Mumba

[= SENEGALIA POLYACANTHA] A. *Senega* subsp. *polyacantha*; a medium-sized to large deciduous tree. H 20m, S 15m, with a straight trunk, upward-spreading branches, and an open, leafy, layered crown. Widespread but relatively short-lived, often a pioneer species invading degraded land. Typically of low and medium altitudes in wooded grassland, dambos and valleys. **Bark:** Yellowish-brown, flaking in corky blocks or loose strips, with woody bosses. Hooked thorns most evident on young branches. Exudes a gum when damaged. **Leaves:** Alternate, compound, bipinnate, < 24cm, with 15–40 pairs of opposite pinnae, middle pinnae largest, with 20–60 pairs of small, triangular leaflets 3 × 0.5mm, light green. Petiole short 0.5–4cm. **Flowers:** Sep–Dec, long spikes < 12cm, white, fragrant, with the new leaves. **Fruit:** Jun–Oct, in bunches at branch ends, a straight, thin, woody dehiscent pod, 7–18cm, dark brown, tapering both ends, slightly curved, splitting to release 6–8 flat, brown seeds. **Notes:** Flowers attract bees. Gum is useful in dyeing and as a pottery pigment. Pods and bark high in protein, browsed by herbivores. A nitrogen-fixing plant. **Other species:** 27 in Zambia, and 8 subspecies now separated into 14 *Vachellia* species (pom-pom flowers) and 13 *Senegalia* species (spiked flowers).

BEST SEEN
Disturbed plateau woodland and most national parks

136   WHITE THORN   Legume Family – Fabaceae

Guidelines for tree identification

  - Determine **which** of the five groups best describes the tree you wish to identify. Match the characteristics to the relevant group. (You may need to break off a leaf or branchlet to check for latex or resin, but remember that it is illegal to damage vegetation in national parks.)
  - Consider **where** you are in Zambia. (Is it wet/dry, high/low altitude?) Study the distribution maps of species that are a possible match.
  - Establish in which **vegetation type** you are. (See map on page 6.)
  - Ask for the **local name** and compare it with the names in the account.

TREE GROUPS IN THIS BOOK

Characteristics of families and genera within each group

GROUP 1 Palms	
ARECACEAE *Borassus, Hyphaene, Phoenix, Raphia*	Trees; **leaves very large**, fan-like, in terminal rosettes with numerous pinnae; dioecious; fruit a soft and edible drupe (*Borassus, Phoenix*), or a large, hard capsule (*Hyphaene, Raphia*).
GROUP 2 Trees that exude milky or watery sap or latex when damaged	
ANACARDIACEAE *Lannea, Ozoroa, Sclerocarya, Searsia*	Diverse family of trees/shrubs, often with watery latex (usually poisonous); leaves usually **compound, imparipinnate**, sometimes **simple and opposite**; usually dioecious; fruit a drupe.
APOCYNACEAE Subfamily Apocynoideae *Holarrhena* Subfamily Rauvolfioideae *Diplorhynchus, Rauvolfia*	Large family of trees/shrubs/lianas/(rarely) herbs, often with poisonous **milky** latex; leaves **simple, opposite or whorled**; usually monoecious; fruit a berry, drupe, or follicle; seeds often winged.
BURSERACEAE *Commiphora*	Trees or shrubs, sometimes **spiny**, leaves and/or bark with milky aromatic resin; leaves usually at branch ends, **simple, alternate** or compound, **imparipinnate**, or **1-** or **2-foliate**; generally dioecious; fruit a drupe.
CLUSIACEAE *Garcinia*	Diverse family of trees/shrubs/herbs, sometimes with yellow/orange latex; leaves **simple, opposite**, subopposite, or **whorled**; monoecious; fruit a capsule, berry or drupe.
EUPHORBIACEAE *Croton, Euphorbia, Schinziophyton*	Large family of trees/shrubs/herbs, usually with milky latex; leaves usually **simple, alternate**, rarely opposite or whorled, **sometimes cactus-like, lobed or compound**; monoecious or dioecious; fruit a capsule, or drupe.
MORACEAE *Ficus*	A diverse family of trees, shrubs and herbs with **milky** or watery latex; leaves alternate, rarely subopposite or whorled, lobed or unlobed; fig fleshy, sometimes edible.
GROUP 3 Trees with simple, mainly opposite (sometimes spiralled or whorled) leaf arrangements	
COMBRETACEAE *Combretum, Terminalia*	Trees/shrubs/climbers/suffrutices; leaves **simple, mainly opposite**, subopposite, or **whorled**; monoecious; fruit 2–5-winged capsule.
LAMIACEAE *Vitex*	Trees/shrubs/perennial herbs, usually with square stems; leaves **simple,** some compound, **opposite, or whorled**; fruit drupes or nuts.
LOGANIACEAE *Strychnos*	Trees/shrubs/lianas; leaves **simple, opposite**, or in whorls of 3, **3–5-veined** from the base; fruit large, round, some edible.
MYRTACEAE *Syzygium*	Trees/shrubs/suffrutices; leaves **simple, usually opposite**, or subopposite, **evergreen**; fruit red, ovoid, fleshy and edible berry or drupe.
OLEACEAE *Schrebera*	Trees/shrubs/climbers/suffrutices; leaves **simple, opposite**, sometimes whorled or alternate; seeds sometimes winged.
RUBIACEAE *Afrocanthium, Breonadia, Canthium, Feretia, Gardenia, Vangueriopsis*	Large family trees/shrubs/climbers/herbs; leaves **simple, opposite, or in whorls**, entire, with **interpetiolar stipules**; fruit a capsule, berry, or drupe, some edible.

GROUP 4 Trees with simple, mainly alternate (sometimes digitate, clustered or spiralled) leaf arrangements	
ANISOPHYLLEACEAE *Anisophyllea*	Trees/shrubs, often accumulating aluminium; leaves **simple**, **spiralled**, or **alternate**; fruit an edible drupe.
ARALIACEAE *Cussonia*	Trees/shrubs/lianas; leaves **simple**, **alternate**, or **compound** (**digitate** or pinnate); generally monoecious; fruit a berry or drupe.
BORAGINACEAE *Cordia*	Trees/shrubs/herbs; leaves **simple**, **alternate**, rarely opposite, or subopposite, **rough textured**; fruit a drupe, or nutlets.
CANNABACEAE *Trema*	Trees/shrubs/herbs, sometimes **spiny**; leaves **simple**, **alternate**, or rarely opposite, **usually 3-veined** from the base; fruit a small drupe.
CHRYSOBALANACEAE *Parinari*	Trees/shrubs/suffrutices; leaves **simple**, **alternate**; monoecious; fruit an edible drupe.
DIPTEROCARPACEAE *Marquesia*, *Monotes*	Trees/ shrubs; leaves **simple**, **alternate**; monoecious; fruit a 1-seeded, indehiscent capsule surrounded by 5-winged drying calyx.
EBENACEAE *Diospyros*	Trees/shrubs/suffrutices; leaves **simple**, usually **alternate**, sometimes opposite, subopposite, or **whorled**; fruit usually a berry.
MALVACEAE	Diverse group of trees/shrubs/herbs whose taxonomy is still under discussion.
Subfamily Bombacioideae *Adansonia*	Trees with swollen trunks; leaves **simple**, **alternate**, or **digitate**; monoecious; fruit a woody capsule.
Subfamily Malvoideae *Thespesia* (= *Azanza*)	Trees/shrubs/herbs; leaves alternate, simple, and 3–7-veined from the base; monoecious; fruit a 4- or 5-lobed dehiscent capsule, some edible.
Subfamily Sterculioideae *Dombeya*, *Sterculia*	Trees/shrubs/herbs; leaves usually alternate, simple or digitately compound; monoecious or dioecious; fruit a capsule or follicle.
OCHNACEAE *Ochna*	Trees/shrubs; leaves **simple**, **alternate**, or **whorled**, often **parallel veined**; monoecious; fruit a 1-seeded drupe.
OLACACEAE *Ximenia*	Trees or shrubs, sometimes **armed**; leaves **simple**, entire, **alternate**; fruit a 1-seeded drupe.
PHYLLANTHACEAE *Bridelia*, *Pseudolachnostylis*, *Uapaca*	Trees/shrubs; leaves **simple**, **alternate**, rarely opposite; fruit a small capsule, drupe, or berry, some edible.
POLYGALACEAE *Securidaca*	Small trees, shrubs or perennial herbs; leaves **simple**, entire, **alternate**; fruit a sometimes winged capsule.
PROTEACEAE *Faurea*, *Protea*	Trees, shrubs or suffrutices; leaves **simple**, entire, **alternate**; fruit a capsule, drupe or nut.
RHAMNACEAE *Phyllogeiton*, *Ziziphus*	Trees, shrubs, suffrutices or lianas, sometimes **thorny**; leaves **simple**, **alternate**, sometimes opposite, or subopposite; fruit a drupe or capsule, some edible.
SALICACEAE *Flacourtia*, *Oncoba*	Deciduous trees/shrubs, frequently riverine, sometimes separated into several subfamilies; leaves **simple**, **alternate**, **toothed**, lanceolate or ovate; fruit a small capsule, or drupe.

Elephants in Luangwa River lagoon

GROUP 5 Trees with compound leaves	
5.1 Compound with 2 or 3 leaflets in various arrangements	
BALANITACEAE *Balanites*	Trees or shrubs; **spiny**; leaves **compound** with **paired asymmetrical leaflets**; fruit a leathery drupe.
FABACEAE **Subfamily Caesalpinioideae** *Colophospermum, Guibourtia*	A large family of trees/shrubs/climbers/herbs common in Miombo woodland; leaves **alternate**, **compound** with **paired asymmetrical leaflets**; fruit a leathery or woody pod.
5.2 Compound with a single terminal leaflet (imparipinnate)	
BIGNONIACEAE *Jacaranda* (exotic), *Kigelia, Markhamia, Spathodia* (exotic), *Stereospermum*	Trees/shrubs/climbers; leaves **compound**, **imparipinnate**, opposite, or whorled; monoecious; flowers often large and **colourful**; fruit a slender capsule (often dehiscent with winged seeds) or a large fruit.
KIRKIACEAE *Kirkia*	Leaves **compound**, **imparipinnate**, **alternate**; monoecious; fruit a small, dehiscent, 4-angled capsule.
MELIACEAE *Trichilia*	Diverse family of trees and shrubs; leaves **simple**, **alternate**, or **compound**, **paripinnate**, or **compound imparipinnate** (opposite or subopposite leaflets); fruit a capsule (some with winged seeds), or drupe.

5.3 Compound, usually paripinnate	
FABACEAE	A large family of trees/shrubs/climbers/herbs common in Miombo woodland.
Subfamily Caesalpinioideae *Afzelia, Baikiaea, Bauhinia, Brachystegia, Burkea, Cassia, Cryptosepalum, Daniellia, Delonix* (exotic), *Erythrophleum, Isoberlinia, Julbernardia, Peltophorum, Piliostigma, Senna, Tamarindus*	Leaves **alternate**, **compound**, **usually paripinnate**, or **lobed**, sometimes bipinnate; fruit a pod, often dehiscent; seeds usually without an areole. Miombo dominant genera are *Brachystegia, Julbernardia* and *Isoberlinia. Brachystegia* species are most easily differentiated by having either few, or many leaflets (*B. allenii, B. bussei, B. floribunda, B. manga, B. spiciformis* and *B. utilis.*) *Julbernardia* species have a distinctive fringe of fine hairs around the margin of the leaflets.
Subfamily Papilionoideae *Baphia, Bobgunnia, Bolusanthus, Cordyla, Craibia, Dalbergia, Dalbergiella, Erythrina, Pericopsis, Philenoptera, Pterocarpus, Xerodderris*	Leaves **alternate**, **compound**, usually **1-pinnate**, or **trifoliate**; fruit a variety of pods; seeds without areoles.
MELIACEAE *Entandrophragma, Khaya*	Diverse family of trees and shrubs; leaves **simple**, **alternate**, or **compound**, **paripinnate**, or **compound**, **imparipinnate** (opposite or subopposite leaflets); fruit a capsule (some with winged seeds), or drupe.
5.4 Compound, bipinnate	
FABACEAE **Subfamily Mimosoideae** * *Acacia* (= *Senegalia, Vachellia*), *Albizia, Amblygonocarpus, Dichrostachys, Entada, Faidherbia, Parkia*	Large family of trees/shrubs/climbers/herbs, common in Miombo woodland; leaves **compound**, **alternate**, **bipinnate**; fruit a pod, or capsule; seeds often with an areole. *Senegalia* species are recognised by spiky inflorescences and usually curved prickles (thorns); the inflorescences in *Vachellia* species are fluffy balls (heads) and they generally have straight spines. *Albizia* species are differentiated by small (*A. amara* and *A. harveyi*), or larger (*A. adianthifolia, A. antunesiana* and *A. versicolor*) leaflets.

* In 2005, the genus *Acacia* was retained for Australian species and in Africa it was split into two genera: *Senegalia* and *Vachellia*. However, in Africa, many people still prefer to use the well-known name *Acacia*. Species of *Acacia* in this book give the new genus name at the start of the description.

- ■ *Senegalia* species have flowers that are borne in spikes and usually have curved prickles (thorns) *Acacia galpinii, A. nigrescens, A. polyacantha*
- ■ *Vachellia* species have spherical flowers and generally have straight spines *Acacia karroo, A. nilotica, A. robusta, A. seyal, A. sieberiana, A. tortilis*

Acacia sieberiana (= *Vachellia sieberiana*) beside Luangwa River

GLOSSARY

annual rings raised ridges representing annual growth stages

ant gall swelling on a plant stem, initiated by parasite activity, colonised by ants

aril external and often-colourful covering on a seed

axillary arising from the angle between the leaf and the stem

boss raised part, often with spines, on a tree trunk

buttress extended ridges at the base of a trunk, providing support

calyx outer sepals of a flower, sometimes retained on the fruit

deciduous shedding leaves annually, usually in the dry season

dehiscent splitting or opening when ripe. Compare **indehiscent**.

dioecious with male and female flowers on different individual plants. Compare **monoecious**.

endocarp seed covering

entire uninterrupted (leaf margin), without teeth or lobes

fissure longitudinal crack in bark

gallery forest forest with a high, gallery-like canopy

ghost tree a tall, white-barked, leafless tree

glaucous grey-green; also a pale waxy bloom, often on a leaf or pod

GMA Game Management Area

herb any plant that is not woody

indehiscent not splitting or opening when ripe. Compare **dehiscent**.

jesse thicket diverse, layered, often spiny thicket on deep sands, derived from dry deciduous forest

lenticel circular pore, often with corky texture, on stems, branches or roots, enabling gas exchange with internal tissues

monoecious with both male and female flowers on the same plant (= bisexual). Compare **dioecious**.

mushitu riparian, evergreen forest

oblanceolate lance-shaped, but with the broadest part at the tip

obovate egg-shaped, but with the broadest part at the tip

palmate divided into segments, hand-shaped (leaf form)

pinna (pl. **pinnae**) primary division/s of a compound leaf off rachis

prickle a sharp, straight or curved, removable armament on a branch or leaf, derived from stem material

rachis the basal leaf axis on which leaflets are arranged

rain tree tree species hosting the larval stage of spittle bugs, which transform the tree sap into a nest of foam 'raining' from the tree

relict referring to a species or forest ecosystem surviving from an earlier geological period

riparian along a river or stream

saponin a chemical compound generating a soapy foam

secondary growth the natural regrowth of woodland after clearing

shrub a small (< 2m) woody plant, usually multi-stemmed

spine a sharp-pointed, hardened armament, being a modified leaf

stigma receptive female part of the flower to which pollen attaches

stipule leaf-like appendage, usually in pairs at the base of a petiole

suffrutex (pl. **suffrutices**) a ground-hugging shrub with leaves and flowers arising from a woody underground stem

thorn a sharp-pointed, hardened armament, being a modified stem

tragacanth resin exuded by a shrub, used in medicine in the Middle East. A similar resin is produced by several African trees.

whorl form in which leaves or other parts arise from the same point

STEM AND LEAF PARTS

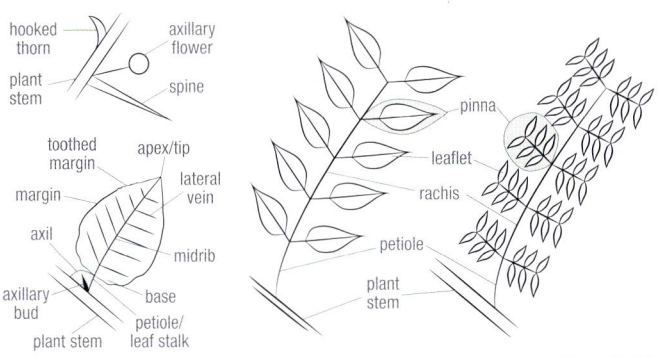

LEAF ARRANGEMENTS

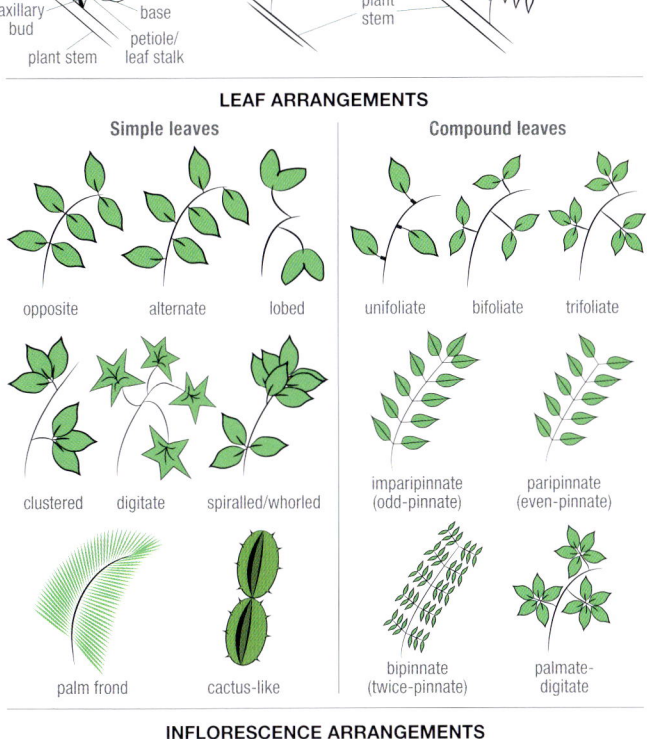

Simple leaves

opposite   alternate   lobed

clustered   digitate   spiralled/whorled

palm frond   cactus-like

Compound leaves

unifoliate   bifoliate   trifoliate

imparipinnate (odd-pinnate)   paripinnate (even-pinnate)

bipinnate (twice-pinnate)   palmate-digitate

INFLORESCENCE ARRANGEMENTS

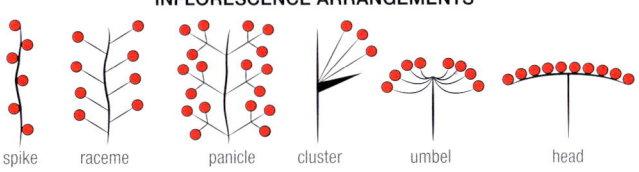

spike   raceme   panicle   cluster   umbel   head

Borassus aethiopum Borassus Palm

LOCAL NAMES: Chibangalala, Chipampa, Muhuma, Kambili, Mulala, Kahuma

Tall fan palm, H 24m, S 6–7m, solitary or in stands; dioecious. Usually unbranched, with 20–30 living and dead leaves, base swollen; swelling also further up the stem; without fibrous roots. Slow-growing, with vertical growth after ± 10 years, only flowering after 30–40 years, thus potentially vulnerable. Widespread on sandy soils in riparian, Munga and Kalahari woodland, dambo margins and around hot springs. **Bark:** Grey to grey-black, smooth with annual rings. **Leaves:** Grey-green fans, 4m, with 50–80 segments joined for half their length. Petiole has hooked spines. **Flowers:** Sep–Oct; male creamy-brown, in

large branching spikes, 0.5–2m; female yellow-green, on 1 or 2 branches, < 2m. **Fruit:** Aug–Nov, in drooping clusters, round, 12–18cm, greenish-yellow or orange. **Notes:** Wood fibrous, termite-resistant, used for dugouts. Seedlings, leading shoots and fruit eaten as a vegetable. Leaves used for mats, fish traps and nets. Flowers and sap used in palm wine. Roots, shoots and fruit have medicinal properties. **Other species:** 4 in the tropics. Occurs with similar *Hyphaene petersiana*, which has smaller, asymmetrical leaves and a base of fibrous roots.

BEST SEEN
Most valley
national parks

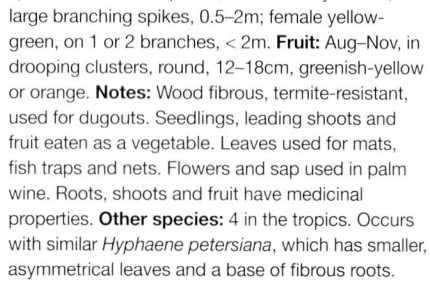

Hyphaene petersiana Hyphaene Palm

Tall fan palm, H 18m, S 7m, solitary or in stands; dioecious. Usually unbranched, with 12–24 living and dead leaves, stem often with swelling just below the crown, base a mass of raised fibrous roots. Widespread in the south on alluvial soils, termite mounds, dambo margins and Kalahari Sand. **Bark:** Grey-black, vertically cracked, with annual rings. **Leaves:** Spiralled, grey-green fans, 1.5–2.5m, waxy, with 20–50 partly joined segments. Petiole and midrib with hooked black spines. **Flowers:** Sep–Nov; males in tangled velvety-brown spikes; females in large, branched sprays with multiple greenish flowers. **Fruit:** Aug–Nov, 4–5cm, round, glossy orange-red to dark brown. Seed inside, hard and white, outer pulp fibrous, sweet and ginger-flavoured. **Notes:** Wood borer-proof, can be polished to a high-gloss finish, used for construction and curios. Shoots eaten as a vegetable. Leaves used for string, baskets and mats. Seeds carved into buttons and curios. ('Vegetable ivory' is a sensible alternative to elephant ivory.) The sap is used to produce palm wine. **Other species:** 9 in the tropics. Sometimes occurs with *Borassus aethiopum*, which has larger symmetrical leaves and trunk not on visible roots.

BEST SEEN
Sandy soils in South Luangwa, Lower Zambezi, Lochinvar, also around hot springs

Phoenix reclinata Wild Date Palm

LOCAL NAMES: Kanchindu, Kanchinda, Kisonga, Chisonga

A spreading palm, H 12m, S 10m, often in clumped stands; dioecious. Stem straight, curving or multi-branched, with 10–50 living and dead leaves crowded on top of stems. Widespread in riverine, swamp or floodplain communities, usually on termite mounds, also in Munga or Kalahari woodland. **Bark:** Blackish, smooth, with concentric leaf scars. **Leaves:** Pinnate, 3–4m, dark green, with 100–200 glossy lanceolate leaflets with sharp tips. **Flowers:** Sep–Nov, both sexes cream-coloured; male on short spikes producing much dust-like pollen; female on long wavy sprays in a hard yellow case that splits open. **Fruit:** Feb–

Apr, in pendulous clusters, ovoid, 1.5cm, orange to reddish-brown, fleshy and date-like, edible. **Notes:** Timber is termite-resistant. Leaves used for mats and rope, mature leaf midribs for baskets. Sap is tapped for palm wine. An easy-to-grow garden plant. **Other species:** None in Zambia, 15 in the tropics, 1 in Europe.

BEST SEEN
Riverine, swampy and floodplain habitats, in most national parks

Raphia farinifera **Raffia Palm**

LOCAL NAMES: Chibale, Mudidi

A short-stemmed palm, H 24m, S 4–10m, with crown of 20–30 arching leaves, and roots from the lower stem; monoecious. Restricted to hot springs, swamp forests, peat swamps and riparian woodland, often in stands. **Bark:** Blackish, with fine vertical fissures. **Leaves:** Tapered fans from the stem, pinnate, 9–18m, green, with long, narrow, glossy leaflets, margins and midribs spiny. Petiole 2m, yellow-brown, smooth. **Flowers:** Oct–Nov, in branched, cream-coloured, plume-like structures, 3m; male flowers above and female flowers below, taking 3 years to form. **Fruit:** Jul–Aug, pine-cone-like, 9cm, with glossy brown scales over a single seed. A short-lived palm (< 35 years), flowering and fruiting in the last 3 years, spreading seeds before collapsing. **Notes:** Leaf stalks used as punting sticks; leaflets for baskets, fish traps and bag-making. Polish made from leaf wax. Sap tapped for palm wine. **Other species:** ± 19, mostly in the tropics.

BEST SEEN

Northern and central headwater swamps; Bangweulu GMA, Lusenga Plain, Lavushi Manda, Kasanka, West Lunga

Lannea discolor **Live-long**

A medium-sized deciduous tree, H 15m, S 8m, with a straight trunk and spreading branches; dioecious. Widespread at lower altitudes in Kalahari, Miombo and Munga woodland, unlikely in evergreen forest. **Bark:** Pale grey to grey-brown, with vertical fissures and ridges. Exudes gum. **Leaves:** At twig ends, alternate, compound, imparipinnate, with 2–5 opposite pairs of leaflets, 6 x 3.5cm, dark green, lighter and hairy below. **Flowers:** Aug–Sep, before new leaves; both on long spikes, 23cm, yellowish and fragrant. **Fruit:** Oct–Nov, along the flower spike, oblong, 10mm, red to purplish, fleshy,

with 2 'horns'. **Notes:** Light wood used for fishing floats. Bark makes good twine. Fruit is edible but with bitter skin, favoured by wildlife; it also has medicinal properties. Roots retain drinkable water. A resilient tree, hence the common name. Propagated easily from truncheons. **Other species:** 9 in Zambia and 4 varieties. *L. schweinfurthii* is similar, but has smoother bark, and leaflets are lanceolate and not lighter below.

BEST SEEN
Open plateaus and escarpment woodlands, Kafue, Lower Zambezi escarpment

Ozoroa reticulata Raisin Tree

A medium-sized semi-deciduous tree, H 14m, S 6–8m, with a twisted, fluted trunk and rounded crown. Occasional in open, dry, Kalahari, Miombo or Munga woodland, but not west of the Zambezi or in evergreen forest. **Bark:** Light brown becoming darker, rough, scaly and horizontally fissured; branchlets hairy. Exudes a creamy resin when damaged. **Leaves:** Simple, either alternate, opposite, or spirally arranged in groups of 3, elliptical, variable in size, 14 x 5cm, dark green, leathery, with distinctive parallel veins. **Flowers:** Nov–Feb, in branched terminal heads, < 17cm, small, cream to white. **Fruit:** Jan–Jun, 10mm, kidney-shaped, glossy black and raisin-like, a single seed. **Notes:** Wood is dark red, a striking material for carving and furniture. Although it is used medicinally for stomach disorders, it may be lethal if overdosed. Good specimen tree, prone to borer attack. **Other species:** 11 in Zambia, 3 varieties: all in Zambia are suffrutices (ground-hugging shrubs, thought to have evolved this way to survive droughts and fires).

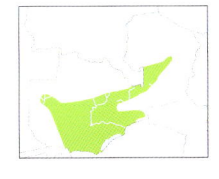

BEST SEEN
Open plateau woodland and central, southern and western national parks

Sclerocarya birrea **Marula**

LOCAL NAMES: Musebe, Muongo, Mulula, Msewe

IN ZAMBIA SUBSP. *CAFFRA*: a medium-sized deciduous tree, H 18m, S 6–10m, with an erect trunk and spreading branches; dioecious. In all dry woodland, at low and medium altitudes, except in Luapula and Northern provinces. **Bark:** Pale grey to grey-brown outside, pink inside; surface is rough with raised scales. Exudes a clear gum. **Leaves:** Crowded in spirals at branch ends, compound, imparipinnate, with 3–7 pairs of opposite, ovate-elliptical leaflets, 6 x 2.5cm, darkish green above, lighter and bluish below, margins sometimes toothed. **Flowers:** Sep–Nov; males in unbranched, 5–8cm sprays, yellow or pink; females

small, on 3cm-long stalks, in groups, red sepals, yellowish petals. **Fruit:** Mar–Jun, a spherical fleshy drupe, 3–4cm, ripening to yellow. 'Eye' markings on seed may indicate the sex of the seed (3 male, 5 female). **Notes:** Flowers attract bees. Edible fruits are favoured by mammals and birds. Rich in vitamin C, used for jam and drinks. Seeds rich in protein; their oil is used in cosmetics. Good specimen tree in gardens. **Other species:** 4 in tropical and southern Africa. The similar *Kirkia acuminata* has more pointed and lanceolate leaflets. *Stereospermum kunthianum* has 2–4 pairs of leaflets.

BEST SEEN
All low-altitude woodlands and valley national parks

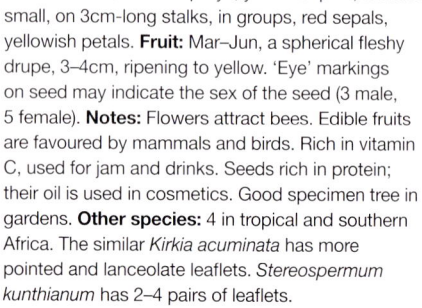

Searsia longipes Large-leaf Rhus

LOCAL NAMES: **Kasalasha, Namulalusha, Chisitu, Chimwamanzi, Mtatatu**

IN ZAMBIA VAR. *LONGIPES*: a small semi-deciduous tree, H 9m, S 3–5m, with a dense, spreading crown, and twigs with yellow hairs. Occasional throughout in open, dry Miombo, Munga or Kalahari woodland, except in the southwest; mainly in secondary growth riparian and montane forest. **Bark:** Creamy-brown and smooth, but with vertical cracks and flaking in strips. **Leaves:** Alternate, compound, trifoliate, elliptical with terminal leaflet larger, 8 x 6cm, and more obovate, darkish green. Petiole short and leathery. Young leaflets apple-green. **Flowers:** Jul–Mar, in drooping clusters (24cm) of loose terminal heads (8cm), small, yellow and fragrant. **Fruit:** Feb–Nov, a round, raisin-like berry, 6–7mm, glossy reddish-brown. **Notes:** A favoured leaf-browse for wildlife, also attracts bees. Fruit is edible and favoured by birds. A possible garden tree attracting wildlife, popular as a screening plant; easily propagated and fast-growing. **Other species:** 11 in Zambia, and 2 varieties: *S. anchietae* has more lanceolate terminal leaflets; *S. lancea* is riverine, with long lanceolate leaflets, < 12cm. May be confused with *Allophyllus africanus*, which has toothed leaflets and also grows on termite mounds.

BEST SEEN
Plateau streams, North and South Luangwa, Lower Zambezi, Kafue

Holarrhena pubescens Jasmine Tree

LOCAL NAMES: Mwenge-busyilu, Mpala-mtowasilu, Mpondasilu, Mbeza-munku

A small semi-evergreen tree, H 2–5m, S 2–3m. Occurs widely below 1,000m, often in rocky, sandy or alluvial soils. **Bark:** Pale grey-brown becoming dark brown, smooth becoming corky, cracked and fissured. Exudes a milky latex if damaged. **Leaves:** Simple, opposite, elliptical to ovate, 10 x 5.5cm, glossy green above, paler below, margin wavy. **Flowers:** Nov–Jan, showy, in dense axillary racemes at branch ends, 1.5–2cm, white and jasmine-scented. **Fruit:** Feb–Jun, very long and slender, paired capsules, < 30 x 0.5cm, splitting to release many 1cm seeds

with parachute-like tuft of silky hairs for wind dispersal. **Notes:** Bark used to treat fevers. A good specimen tree in domestic gardens, planted in groups; can be difficult to propagate. **Other species:** None in Zambia; 4 in tropical Africa. Often associated with *Combretum*, *Terminalia*, *Burkea* and *Markhamia* thickets.

BEST SEEN
Low-altitude thickets on sandy and alluvial soils; in most national parks

Diplorhynchus condylocarpon **Rubber Pod Tree**

LOCAL NAMES: Mwenge, Mulya, Muzi, Mtowa, Mutowa

An untidy semi-deciduous tree, H 11m, S 4–6m, often multi-stemmed, with drooping branches and spreading crown. A widespread, fire-tolerant species in most woodland types except canopy forests, often in rocky locations.
Bark: Red-brown becoming darker, rough and corky, with fissures like crocodile skin; branchlets with lenticels. Bark and pods exude white latex when damaged.
Leaves: Drooping at branch ends, simple, opposite, elliptical, 6 x 3.5cm, yellow-green, leathery, slightly hairy. Petiole 3cm. **Flowers:** Aug–Nov, in loose, few-flowered, axillary panicles, 10mm, white and scented. **Fruit:** Jun–Aug, twin curved pods, 2–5cm, grey-brown, leathery with small warts. Skin splits to release 2–4 winged seeds.
Notes: Wood usually small, pale; good firewood. Rolled leaves used to mimic antelope calls. Latex is good birdlime and chewing gum. Roots used to treat stomach problems and snakebite. **Other species:** A single-species genus in tropical Africa.

BEST SEEN
Miombo woodland on escarpments and plateaus, most national parks

Rauvolfia caffra Quinine Tree

LOCAL NAMES: Mwimbi, Mubimbi, Mutoto, Mvumbamvula

A tall, dense evergreen tree, H 24m, S 5–15m, with a rounded crown and drooping branches in whorls of four. Widespread in riverine or wet woodland and forest, except in the dry southwest. **Bark:** Dark yellow-brown or dark grey and rough with fine, even-ridged squares. Exudes copious toxic white latex when damaged. **Leaves:** Mango-like at branch ends, simple, opposite, or in whorls of 3–5, narrowly lanceolate, 8–12 x 3–6cm, darkish glossy green and leathery, with distinctively pale midrib. **Flowers:** Jul–Oct, in showy terminal sprays (cymes) 12–20cm, small, 4mm, creamy and fragrant. **Fruit:** Nov–Feb,

in clusters, round, 2-lobed and grape-sized, 2cm, green becoming purple, with 1 or 2 grooved seeds. **Notes:** Secretions from froghoppers (spittle bugs) produce a 'rain tree' effect. A good firewood and shade tree. Seeds contain numerous alkaloids, but to date without commercial uses. Fast-growing from seed or truncheons. **Other species:** 1 other species in Zambia: *R. nana* reported from western Zambia. *R. caffra* is similar to another riverine species, *Breonardia salicina*, which is confined to the east, and without milky latex.

BEST SEEN
Escarpment and plateaus along Miombo streams in most national parks except Sioma Ngwezi and Liuwa Plain

Commiphora marlothii   Paper-bark Corkwood

A small to medium-sized deciduous tree without spines, H 7m, S 2–5m, with multiple branches giving a rounded crown when in leaf. Generally leafless Apr–Oct. Widespread at lower altitudes on rocky ground and in Munga woodland, often on termite mounds. **Bark:** Papery, aromatic and peeling in large sheets revealing green under-bark, becoming dark brown and scaly. Branchlets hairy. Exudes a white sticky gum when damaged. **Leaves:** Alternate, compound, imparipinnate with 3 or 4 pairs of oblong-obovate leaflets, 5 x 3cm, pale green with paler underside, both sides finely hairy, margins toothed, aromatic when crushed. Petiole 10cm. **Flowers:** Oct–Nov, in small axillary clusters, 4–15cm, inconspicuous, yellow. Before the new leaves. **Fruit:** Nov–Mar, fleshy, ovoid, 1cm, with a pointed tip, changing from green to red. Skin splits revealing a single seed attached by a bright red, 3- or 4-lobed pseudo-aril in mucilaginous, aromatic flesh. **Notes:** Charcoal has been used for gunpowder. Fascinating specimen tree. **Other species:** 16 in Zambia, difficult to distinguish. *C. mollis* is most similar, also without spines, but leaflets are ovate-elliptical, without toothed margins.

BEST SEEN
Luangwa and Zambezi valley escarpments and Munga woodlands

Garcinia livingstonei African Mangosteen

LOCAL NAMES: Mulyanganga, Chipufwe, Muchindu, Mumpili, Mukonongo

An evergreen tree, H 18m, S 4–6m, with distinctive spiny branching; dioecious. Widespread across the southern half of Zambia at lower altitudes, but also in the Copperbelt and Northern provinces, mainly in riparian woodland, limestone sinkholes, and on termite mounds in Munga and Mopane woodland. **Bark:** Dark grey or brown, becoming darker with age, with vertical fissures. Exudes a thick yellow or red latex when damaged, that stains. **Leaves:** Usually on short spurs, simple, opposite or whorled in threes, 4–14 x 1.5–11cm, elliptical, glossy dark green, leathery, with a prominent pale

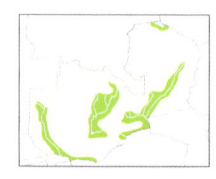

midrib and wavy margins. **Flowers:** Jul–Sep, in clusters at short branch nodes, with creamy-green petals and a sickly-sweet scent. **Fruit:** Sep–Nov, a round drupe, 2.5cm, orange when ripe, edible. Produces up to 5 seeds. **Notes:** Bark and roots used as an aphrodisiac and to reduce pregnancy pain. Leaves and flowers have antibiotic properties. Latex provides an adhesive gum. Fruit enjoyed by wildlife and numerous frugivorous birds; also produces a porridge or fermented drink. Unusual specimen tree attracting birds. **Other species:** 8 in Zambia, occurring in different habitats. **Near Threatened.**

BEST SEEN
Escarpment
Miombo and most
national parks

Croton gratissimus **Lavender Croton**

A semi-evergreen tree, H 10m, S 4–10m, with distinctive silvery leaf under-surfaces. The trunk is often Y-shaped with whorled branches; young branches are rust-coloured and hairy. Widespread especially in rocky areas along streams. **Bark:** Pale to dark grey, roughish. **Leaves:** Simple, alternate, opposite or spirally arranged, elliptical, variable, 1.5–18 x 0.5–6cm, shiny green above and characteristically silvery below, leathery and aromatic, with a prominent pale midrib and wavy margins. Petiole 0.5–7cm. **Flowers:** Sep–Nov, borne in spikes, < 15cm, predominantly male with a few female flowers at the base, small, 6mm, with yellow petals and sweetly scented.

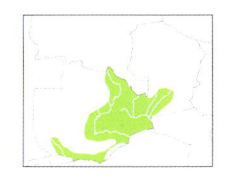

Fruit: Mar–May, a small, 8–11mm, 3-lobed drupe, greenish to orange. **Notes:** An attractive, umbrella-shaped ornamental garden tree, attracting birds and providing dappled shade. **Other species:** 12 other species and subspecies in Zambia. Most similar are *C. macrostachyus* and *C. sylvaticus*, but neither has the distinctly paler underleaf and both are confined to wetter habitats. Other species are constituents of riverine or gallery forest.

BEST SEEN
Eastern, southern and western national parks

Croton megalobotrys   **Fever-berry Croton**

LOCAL NAMES: Mulyanganga, Chimonomono, Munanga, Mukena, Munganga

A shrubby, densely leafy evergreen tree, H 15m, usually 3–5m, S 4–8m, with drooping branches. Occurs widely across the southern river valleys, also in the Luapula River system. **Bark:** Pale grey and smooth, with vertical lines of lenticels. Produces a watery sap when damaged. **Leaves:** Simple, alternate, ovate to almost triangular, 4–18 x 2–13cm, dark green above and paler below, with silvery hairs above and below, 3–7-veined from the base, with sharp apex and toothed margin. Petiole 2–7cm. **Flowers:** Sep–Nov, on terminal spikes, 4.5–17cm, with male and female sometimes on the same spike, greenish-yellow. **Fruit:** Dec–Jan,

a roundish, 3-lobed fleshy capsule, 3–4cm, bright green with white hairs, ripening to brown and woody, not splitting. **Notes:** Wood is light-coloured. Seeds produce oil, reputed to have anti-malarial and other medicinal properties. **Other species:** 12 other species and subspecies in Zambia. Similar species: *C. leuconeurus* with only a single midrib, *C. longipedicellatus* with a long, tapering leaf apex; *C. menyharthii* with lanceolate leaves. Other species are constituents of either riverine or gallery forest.

BEST SEEN
North and South Luangwa, Lower Zambezi, Kafue

Euphorbia ingens Candelabra Tree

A deciduous succulent tree, H 20m, S 6–10m, with a circular trunk, becoming a 4-sided candelabrum with broad 'wings', short, paired spines, and a dense, rounded crown. Occurs widely, often on termite mounds and in Mopane, Munga and Miombo woodland, Itigi thicket and rocky areas. **Bark:** Pale to dark grey-brown, with deep transverse fissures, and vertical flaking. Exudes copious toxic white latex when damaged. **Leaves:** Appearing briefly at the beginning of the rainy season, at branch ends, very small, pale green and fleshy. **Flowers:** Mar–Aug, on the winged margins of terminal branch nodes, small, 6–10mm, yellow-green. **Fruit:** Jul–Sep, a globose, 3-lobed capsule, 1.5cm, green becoming red-brown, edible, releasing 2 round seeds. **Notes:** Stem produces a tough, light wood used for building and burned to create fertiliser. Latex is toxic and highly irritant, but has been used to treat stomach disorders, and also as a fish poison and birdlime. **Other species:** 58 other species and 6 variants in Zambia, mostly succulents: *E. cooperi* and *E. fortissimo* are small spiny trees of low valley areas; *E. tirucalli* is a village hedging plant.

> **BEST SEEN**
> Plateau and escarpment Miombo and Itigi thicket, most national parks

Schinziophyton rautanenii **Mongongo Tree**

A large, stout, spreading deciduous tree, H 20m, S 6–10m, with a circular stem; dioecious. Branchlets have dense rusty hairs. Occurs widely, but more common in the southwest in Kalahari and Munga woodland, sometimes in almost pure stands. **Bark:** Smooth, grey to golden-brown, sometimes peeling. Exudes white latex when damaged. **Leaves:** Spirally arranged, compound, digitate, with 5–7 elliptic to oblanceolate leaflets, < 18 x 9cm, dark green above and greyer below, with tapering apex and base, becoming yellow before falling. **Flowers:** Oct–Nov, in slender sprays or cymes, < 12cm,

small, 10mm, yellow. **Fruit:** Feb–Apr, an ovoid capsule, 3.5 x 2.5cm, grey-green and hairy, with a single hard seed. **Notes:** Wood is pale off-white and light, similar to balsa wood, used for toys and packaging. Seed has an edible kernel yielding a bright yellow oil with commercial value, used in cosmetics. **Other species:** A single species in tropical and southern Africa.

BEST SEEN
Lochinvar, Kafue, Sioma Ngwezi and Liuwa Plain; dry southwestern Kalahari woodlands

Ficus burkei Common Wild Fig

LOCAL NAMES: Kanya-nguni, Mamina-ngoma, Kacele, Mutaba

A medium-sized to large evergreen or semi-deciduous tree, H 15–18m, S 12–25m, with a rounded spreading crown. Sometimes a 'strangler' with aerial roots. Common in moist wooded grassland, on termite mounds and around human habitation. **Bark:** Dark grey to light brown, smooth, sometimes with vertical lines. Exudes white latex when damaged. **Leaves:** Simple, alternate or whorled, elliptical or obovate, 8 x 4cm, light to dark green above, paler below, stiff, leathery, usually hairless. Midrib prominent, no paired basal veins, apex acute, margin entire. Petiole < 8cm. **Flowers:** Year-round, flowering parts are inside a receptacle that becomes the fig, requiring species-specific wasps for pollination. **Fruit:** Most months, in leaf axils, 1 or 2 figs, stalkless, ± 1cm, yellow-green with cream spots, red when mature, sometimes hairy. **Notes:** Bark, latex and fruit have medicinal uses. **Other species:** 36 species and 4 subspecies; habitat-specific; > 700 species of *Ficus* in tropical and warm areas.

BEST SEEN
Most national parks
and woodland types

Ficus bussei **Zambezi Fig**

A very large evergreen or semi-deciduous tree, H 18m, S < 36m, with a wide-spreading, rounded crown. Germinates as a 'strangler' on a host tree, with aerial roots thickening to become supporting pillars. Common on alluvial terraces in major river valleys in the east and south. **Bark:** Grey-brown and roughish, finely longitudinally fissured, flaking in chunks. Exudes white latex when damaged. **Leaves:** Simple, spirally arranged, ovate, oblong or elliptic, < 24 x 8.5cm, dark green above and paler below, velvety, with paired veins from the base, prominent below, apex usually acute, base heavily lobed, and margin entire. Petiole 2–8cm. **Flowers:** Sep–Feb, flowering parts are inside a receptacle that becomes the fig, requiring species-specific wasps for pollination. **Fruit:** Oct–Apr, in leaf axils or clusters on branches, 1 or 2 figs, round with stalks, < 2.5cm, yellow-green with cream spots on raised warts, yellow when ripe, velvety. **Notes:** Latex used to treat conjunctivitis and burns. Fruit eaten by humans and frugivorous birds, bats and monkeys. A good shade tree where space permits, but not frost-hardy. **Other species:** 36 species and 4 subspecies; venation differs and species are often habitat-specific. > 700 species of *Ficus* in tropical and warm areas.

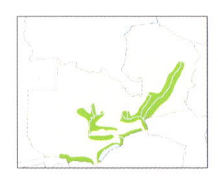

BEST SEEN
Most low-lying valley national parks

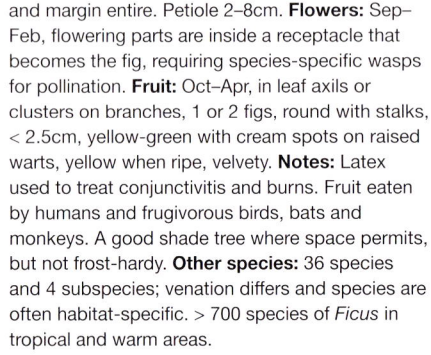

Ficus ingens Red-leaved Rock Fig

LOCAL NAMES: Mupata, Musole, Chilembalemba, Mutata, Muteba

A small to large, free-standing deciduous tree, H 14m, S 30m, with a ribbed trunk and rounded or spreading crown. Occurs in most woodland and wooded grassland habitats, except in the west. Grows on rocky hills and in gorges as a 'rock splitter', sometimes espaliered; also on riversides and termite mounds. **Bark:** Grey-brown and smooth, with lenticels in horizontal lines. Produces copious white latex when damaged. **Leaves:** Simple, alternate, ovate to oblong-lanceolate, 17 x 10cm, shiny dark green above and paler below, hairless, with a distinctive basal pair of lateral veins across lobes to margins, apex rounded or tapering, margin entire and flat or slightly wavy. Petiole short. New leaves distinctively bronze-red. **Flowers:** Jul–Aug and Dec–Jan, flowering parts are inside a receptacle that becomes the fig, requiring species-specific wasps to enter for pollination. **Fruit:** Jun–Dec, round figs in pairs on stalks in leaf axils, 1–1.5cm, yellow, purple when ripe, velvety. **Notes:** Latex used as a disinfectant and glue. Fruit eaten by humans and favoured by frugivorous birds, bats and monkeys. **Other species:** A large genus in Zambia, with 36 species and 4 subspecies; venation differs, and species are often habitat-specific. > 700 species of *Ficus* in tropical and warm areas.

BEST SEEN
In most national parks and rocky valleys, except in the west

Ficus sur Cape Fig

LOCAL NAMES: **Mukunyu, Mukuyu, Kakeke, Namonde**

A large, semi-evergreen tree, H 25m, S < 30m, often with swollen base, heavy branches and roundish spreading crown. Not a strangler. A canopy species in evergreen forest, also widespread in riparian, Munga and other woodlands, sometimes in swamp forest and on rocky hillsides. **Bark:** Grey or creamy-grey, smooth becoming rough and dark, with raised scales. Copious white latex when damaged. **Leaves:** Simple, alternate or spiralled, ovate to elliptical, < 15 x 12cm, shiny dark green above and paler below, hairless, with apex tapering, margins broadly toothed. Petiole < 6cm, grooved. New leaves distinctively scarlet. **Flowers:** Jun–Sep, flowering parts are inside a receptacle that becomes the fig, requiring species-specific wasps to enter for pollination. **Fruit:** Most months, but especially Sep–Mar, round figs in dense branched clusters on the stem, branches and sometimes roots, < 4cm, yellow becoming red, mottled with cream. **Notes:** Wood is soft and light, used for drums. Fruit edible by humans, birds and other animals; tasty in jam, also thought to enhance milk production in cattle. All parts used in traditional medicine. A good shade tree, easy to grow. **Other species:** 36 species and 4 subspecies; venation differs, and species are often habitat-specific. > 700 species of *Ficus* in tropical and warm areas.

BEST SEEN
Most national parks and woodland areas

Ficus sycomorus **Sycomore Fig**

LOCAL NAMES: **Mkunyu, Mukuyu, Katema, Mkuyu**

A large semi-deciduous tree, H 20m, S < 20m, with a short, often-buttressed trunk, spreading branches and dense, roundish crown. Not a strangler. Occurs throughout, frequently in riparian and savanna woodland and in dambo margins, also in Miombo woodland in the north, and around human habitation. **Bark:** Pale yellow-brown to grey, vertically cracked into scales. Produces copious white latex when damaged. **Leaves:** Simple, alternate, or spiralled, ovate to circular, < 17 x 15cm, green, hairy below, rough and harsh to the touch, margin sometimes broadly toothed. Petiole 3cm. **Flowers:** Jun–Sep and Dec–Jan, flowering parts are inside a receptacle that becomes the fig, requiring species-specific wasps to enter for pollination. **Fruit:** Most months, mainly Jul–Dec, figs in dense, branched clusters on the main stem and branches, round, < 3cm, yellow or red when ripe, hairy. **Notes:** Wood soft and light, used for drums. Bark used for making rope. Fruit edible fresh or dried, favoured by herbivores (who also browse the leaves) and frugivorous birds. All parts of the plant are used in traditional medicine. **Other species:** 36 species and 4 subspecies; venation differs, and species are often habitat-specific. > 700 species of *Ficus* in tropical and warm areas. *F. sur* and *F. vallis-choudae* similar but without yellowish bark and rough leaves.

BEST SEEN
Most national parks, common in most habitats

Combretum apiculatum Red Bushwillow

LOCAL NAMES: Kalamafupa, Kapumpa, Kakolo, Manoyonya

IN ZAMBIA SUBSP. *APICULATUM*: a small to medium-sized deciduous tree, H 10m, S 6m, with upward-spreading branches and a narrow, rounded crown. Widespread, usually at low to medium altitudes, often on sandy soils in dry, open woodland. **Bark:** Grey to dark grey-brown, smooth and lumpy, becoming scaly and rough. **Leaves:** Simple, opposite, ovate to elliptical, > 4.5 x 6cm, olive-green, leathery and sometimes hairy, apex rounded but with a sharp tip, margin entire. Petiole 1cm. **Flowers:** Sep–Feb, on slender axillary spikes, < 7cm, small, 5mm, yellow to creamy-green and very fragrant. **Fruit:** Jan–May, round

and 4-winged, 2–3cm, ripening to reddish-brown, hairless. Sometimes remaining on the tree until Nov. **Notes:** Wood is heavy and hard, but rarely used. Leaves and bark are used in traditional medicine to treat stomach disorders. A biodiversity contributor, attracts hornbills, and bees and other insects. **Other species:** 26 other species and 6 subspecies in Zambia; possibly numerous *C. collinum* subspecies. A large genus, with 250 other species across the tropics, but not in Australia.

BEST SEEN
Most national parks and sandy, open woodland

Combretum collinum Weeping Bushwillow

LOCAL NAMES: Mufuka, Mulamana, Kalama, Mkute, Mukunza

A small to medium-sized, semi-deciduous tree, H 19m, S 10m, with upward-spreading branches and a dense, rounded crown. Widespread, common in hilly areas (*collinum* – 'of hill'), deciduous thicket, and Kalahari and Lake Basin Chipya woodland, also in *Baikiaea* forest margins, on termite mounds and in Miombo woodland. **Bark:** Variable, creamy-brown to grey or dark brown, rough, sometimes spirally fissured with smooth scales. **Leaves:** Simple, opposite, variable, elliptic to obovate, < 19 x 8cm, glossy green above, grey and scaly below, tapering to the apex, base rounded. Petiole 1–3cm.

Flowers: Aug–Oct, with the old leaves, in showy, creamy, axillary spikes, 5–10cm, small, 5mm, fragrant. **Fruit:** May–Sep, 4-winged, variable from round to pointed at the apex, 3–5cm, showy, rusty-red to purple when young, ripening to chocolate- or golden-brown, shiny; sometimes on the tree until Nov. **Notes:** Attracting hornbills, bees and other insects. **Other species:** 26 other species and 6 subspecies in Zambia. With 250 other species across the tropics, not in Australia.

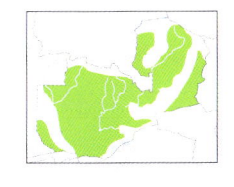

BEST SEEN
Most national parks, escarpments and Kalahari Sand areas

Combretum imberbe Leadwood

OTHER NAMES: **Musimbita, Muzwili, Munyonya, Nyonje, Mubimba**

A large deciduous tree, H 30m, S 20m, with upward-spreading, sometimes drooping branches and an open, rounded crown. Branchlets sometimes spiny, with reddish scales. Occurs in the south and east, usually on sandy soils in Munga and Kalahari woodland, around *Baikiaea* forest margins, and sometimes in Mopane woodland and dambo margins. **Bark:** Pale to dark grey-brown, finely fissured with horizontal cracks and uniform scales. **Leaves:** Simple, opposite, on often-spine-tipped twigs, oval, usually 4 x 2cm, grey-green, leathery and hairless, but with minute silvery scales below, apex

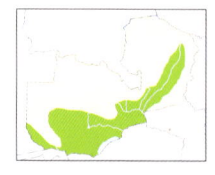

usually tipped and margin wavy. Petiole 1cm. **Flowers:** Nov–Mar, on slender axillary spikes, 4–8cm, 5mm, creamy-yellow and fragrant. **Fruit:** Mar–May, round, 4-winged, 1–2cm, yellow or reddish ripening to pale brown and shiny with silvery scales; sometimes remaining on the tree to Aug. **Notes:** Wood is heavy and hard, historically used for railway sleepers, sometimes reused to make furniture. Flowers attract bees, other insects and birds, especially hornbills. **Other species:** 26 other species and 6 subspecies in Zambia. A large genus, with 250 other species across the tropics, but not in Australia.

BEST SEEN
Valley national parks on alluvial and sandy soils; most common in the south

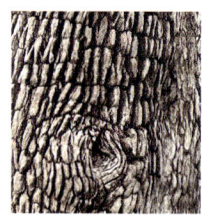

Combretum molle Velvet Bushwillow

A small to medium-sized deciduous tree, H 13m, S 15m, with stem often leaning, and with heavy, drooping branches and an open, rounded crown. Widespread in most woodland types, and most common in Miombo woodland, often on termite mounds; less common in the southwest. **Bark:** Dark black-brown, rough and finely fissured with small, uniformly square scales. **Leaves:** Simple, opposite, variable, ovate-elliptic, usually 8 x 5cm, dull green with dense velvety hairs on both surfaces; all veins distinctly sunken above, tapering to the apex, base rounded. Petiole short and thick, 1cm. **Flowers:** Aug–Nov, in dense, often-branched axillary spikes, 4–9cm, small, 5mm, creamy-yellow to yellow, fragrant. Appearing with the new leaves. **Fruit:** Jun–Sep, 4-winged, small, 1.5–2cm, yellowish-green ripening to reddish. Sometimes remaining on the tree to Nov. **Notes:** An attractive garden tree, favoured by bees and other insects, and birds, especially hornbills and other insect-eating birds. **Other species:** 26 other species and 6 subspecies in Zambia. *C. molle* is a diverse species with much variation. A large genus, with 250 other species across the tropics, but not in Australia.

BEST SEEN
Plateau woodland and Luangwa, Lower Zambezi and Kafue national parks

Combretum zeyheri Large-fruited Bushwillow

LOCAL NAMES: **Mufuka, Mukenge, Musense, Kalamafupa, Mukutabulonga**

A small to medium-sized, often multi-stemmed, semi-deciduous tree, H 15m, S 12m, with upward-reaching branches and an open, rounded crown. Widespread in most woodland types and sandier soils (especially on Kalahari Sand), also in Miombo and Munga woodland, and on termite mounds and rocky outcrops. **Bark:** Grey to pale brown, usually smooth, banded or finely fissured, with small, uniformly square scales, flaking to give a mottled effect. **Leaves:** Simple, opposite, sometimes in whorls of 3, oblong to ovate, 9 x 4cm, yellowish-green, with velvety hairs when young, margin entire and wavy, tapering to the base. Petiole short and thick, 1cm. **Flowers:** Aug–Oct, in dense, often catkin-like axillary spikes, 3–7cm, small, 5mm, creamy-yellow to yellow, and fragrant; appearing with the new leaves, showy in profusion. **Fruit:** May–Sep, 4-winged, conspicuously large, < 9cm, green becoming glossy yellow-brown, the base notched. Often remaining on the tree. **Notes:** Favoured by bees and other insects, and insect-eating birds, especially hornbills. Fibrous roots used for basketry, especially by the Mbunda people. Attractive garden tree. **Other species:** 26 other species and 6 subspecies in Zambia. A large genus, with 250 other species across the tropics, but not in Australia.

BEST SEEN
Most national parks and woodlands, particularly in the southwest

Terminalia sericea Silver-leaf Terminalia

A medium-sized to large, upward-spreading, deciduous tree, H 18m, S 12m, with wavy branches and an open crown. Branchlets dark purple and young stems frequently galled. Widespread on sandy soils in Munga, Kalahari and *Baikiaea* woodland, sometimes in Mopane and Miombo woodland, less common in the north and northwest. **Bark:** Grey and smooth, becoming dark brown, rough and vertically fissured in deep linking furrows with peeling flakes. **Leaves:** Clustered at branch ends, simple, spirally arranged, ovate-elliptical, 6 x 3.5cm, grey-green and leathery, with minute silvery scales below, midrib prominent, base tapering and apex usually tipped.

Petiole < 1cm. **Flowers:** Sep–Dec, in axillary spikes, < 7cm, small, 5mm, creamy to greenish-white, unpleasant-smelling. Appearing with the new leaves. **Fruit:** Jan–May, flat and 2-winged, small, 2.5–3.5cm, pink to reddish, ripening to reddish-brown, sometimes remaining on the tree. **Notes:** Wood yellow and heavy. Bark makes good rope, also yields yellow tannin. Root extracts are used as an eyewash and to treat stomach disorders and pneumonia. Host to butterfly and moth species. **Other species:** 13 other species, subspecies and hybrids in Zambia. A large genus with 150 species across the tropics. *T. prunioides* is similar, but with obovate leaves and plum-red fruit.

BEST SEEN
Most national parks, but especially lower valleys and the west

Terminalia stenostachya Cluster-leaf Terminalia

LOCAL NAMES: Chibowe, Macula-mungonone, Mkukwe, Waukulu

A medium-sized semi-deciduous tree, H 10m, S 8m, with wavy, upward-spreading branches and an open, rounded crown. Branchlets often leaf-scarred. Common in the east and south, typically on sandy soils in Munga, escarpment Miombo and occasionally Mopane woodland, often on termite mounds. **Bark:** Dark grey and rough, with deep, connected, vertical fissures with peeling flakes. **Leaves:** Clustered into rosettes at branch ends, simple, spirally arranged, recurved, oblong to ovate-elliptical, large, 15 x 6cm, dark green, leathery, undersurface hairy, midrib prominent with 12–15 pairs of lateral veins, base and apex rounded. Petiole < 3cm.

Flowers: Sep–Jan, on solitary, delicate axillary spikes, < 14cm, small, 5mm, creamy-white and unpleasant-smelling. **Fruit:** Jan–Jun, usually in the leaf rosette, flat and 2-winged, 4.5–6cm, yellowish to bright red, ripening to reddish brown, hairy. May remain on the tree for some months. **Notes:** Wood is yellowish and heavy. Roots used in traditional medicine. **Other species:** 13 other species, subspecies and hybrids in Zambia; 150 species across the tropics. *T. mollis* similar but without rosetted leaves, with hairy leaf margins and larger yellow fruit in big clusters.

BEST SEEN
Luangwa, Lochinvar, Lower Zambezi and Kafue

Vitex payos Chocolate Berry

A small deciduous tree, H 15m, S 10m, with outward-spreading branches and a rounded or flattened crown. Fairly common in valleys at low and medium altitudes, in open woodland and on termite mounds and rocky slopes. **Bark:** Distinctive, grey-brown and vertically fissured. **Leaves:** Opposite, compound, 5–7-foliate, basal leaflets smaller or absent. Leaflets variable, oblong to obovate, 11 x 3cm, light green above and yellowish below, leathery, finely hairy, with tawny hairs on midrib, base tapering, apex rounded. Petiole straight, 5–15cm. **Flowers:** Aug–Jan, in dense, axillary heads, 6–15cm, small, 6mm, 2-lipped, upper white, lower mauve or blue.

Fruit: Apr–Aug, round, fleshy, 2–2.5cm, purplish-black with a persistent calyx, edible (coffee-flavoured), containing 1 seed. **Notes:** Wood usable, polishes well. Bark can be used as dye for cloth. Leaves and fruit browsed by wildlife. Fruit contains vitamins A and B, makes good jam. **Other species:** 7 other species and 1 subspecies in Zambia, all 3-, 5- or 7-foliate shrubs and small trees. *V. doniana* is similar, but leaves more ovate and nearly hairless, apex sometimes notched and petiole long and curved.

BEST SEEN
Most national parks and woodland areas

Strychnos spinosa Monkey Orange

LOCAL NAMES: Kamino, Katonga, Munkulunkulu, Mtembe, Mzimbili, Muntamba

A small to medium-sized, spiny, deciduous tree, H 9m, S 8m, with upward-spreading branches and an open, rounded crown; dioecious. Widespread in most woodland types and thicket. **Bark:** Grey-brown and rough, flaking in rectangular segments, ringed at the nodes with axillary curved or straight spines in pairs or threes. **Leaves:** Simple, opposite, in pairs or threes, variable, elliptic to almost circular, 4 x 3cm, light to dark green and shiny above, duller below, distinctly 3–7-veined from or near the base. Petiole 2–10mm. **Flowers:** Sep–Nov, in short, dense terminal heads, 4cm, small, 6mm, with variable colours from

white and pale green to yellow. **Fruit:** May–Sep, round, < 12cm, green ripening to yellow, woody, with 10–100 pale seeds in edible pulp. **Notes:** Said to have supernatural properties. Green fruits and roots used as an emetic and snakebite treatment. Dry fruit shell used as a musical instrument. **Other species:** 14 other species in Zambia; 2 are climbers, others are found in riverine situations. Similar to *S. cocculoides*, which has a rounded, non-tapering leaf base, a smaller, dark green fruit and corky bark.

BEST SEEN
Most national parks and woodland areas

Syzygium cordatum Waterberry

LOCAL NAMES: **Mushingu, Musombo, Mutoye, Katope**

A small to medium-sized evergreen tree, H 20m, S 5–10m, with spreading branches and a dense, rounded crown. Widespread, usually close to water, mostly in riparian and swamp forest, also on termite mounds and dambo edges. **Bark:** Red-brown and smooth, becoming dark brown and fissured, producing small scales. **Leaves:** Crowded at branch ends, simple, opposite in pairs, with successive pairs at right angles, elliptic, oblong to almost circular, 6 x 4cm, blue-green above, paler below, leathery. Petiole short. **Flowers:** Jul–Nov, in dense heads at branch ends, 2–2.5cm, creamy-white to pink, sweet-scented, with much nectar. **Fruit:** Nov–Mar, an ovoid berry, 2cm, glossy purple-black and fleshy, with a single whitish seed. **Notes:** Wood is suitable for furniture but stems usually small. Bark produces a blue dye. Leaves and roots used in traditional medicine. Fruit edible, favoured by wildlife and birds. An attractive garden tree planted close to water. **Other species:** 2 other species in Zambia: *S. guineense* with 7 subspecies and *S. owariense*, a tall swamp and evergreen forest tree. A large genus worldwide, taxonomy unresolved.

BEST SEEN
Most national parks and streamlines

Syzygium guineense White-bark Waterberry

LOCAL NAMES: Mufinsa, Musombo, Musompe, Katope

IN ZAMBIA SUBSP. *BAROTSENSE*: a medium-sized evergreen tree, H 12m, S 20m, often multi-stemmed, with wide-spreading branches and an open crown. A distinctive feature on riverbanks and islands in the west. **Bark:** Pale grey and smooth, sometimes buttressed or with aerial roots from the branches. Produces a reddish sap when damaged. **Leaves:** Simple, opposite in pairs, elliptic, 7 x 3cm, glossy green above, paler below, leathery, apex tapering to a point. Petiole short, 1–2cm. **Flowers:** Aug–Nov, 6–8cm, creamy-white with conspicuous stamens in clusters, sweet-scented. **Fruit:** Oct–Jan, in clusters of

20–30, an ovoid berry, 3cm, half white, half purple-black, glossy, with a single whitish seed; seeds float in water. **Notes:** Wood used for furniture and canoes, but splits. Bark produces tannin. Leaves and roots used to bathe sick patients. Fruit edible, favoured by wildlife and birds. Attractive in gardens near water. **Other species:** 2 other species and 7 subspecies in Zambia: see *S. cordatum*. *S. owariense*, a tall swamp and evergreen forest tree. A large genus worldwide, with taxonomy still unresolved.

> **BEST SEEN**
> Kafue, Sioma Ngwezi
> and Liuwa Plain

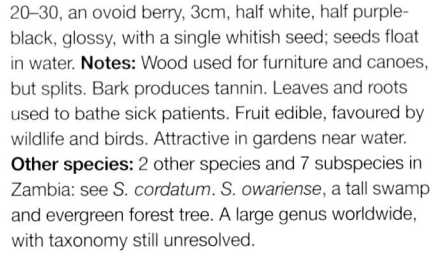

Schrebera trichoclada Wooden Pear

LOCAL NAMES: Kapanda, Mutwanakabaya, Kaoki, Katobwangu, Kampelembenda

A small tree, H 10m, S 5–9m, with branches spreading upwards and outwards, often with drooping ends. Occurring occasionally, mainly on sandy and rocky soils in Munga and Kalahari woodland and, more occasionally, in Miombo and Chipya woodland. **Bark:** Grey or creamy-brown with numerous white lenticels, becoming scaly on the lower stem, flaking in circular patches with age. **Leaves:** Simple, opposite, elliptic to ovate, usually 9 x 5cm, dull green above and paler below, leathery and sometimes hairy, both the base and apex slightly tapering. Petiole 1–1.5cm. **Flowers:** Sep–Jan, axillary or terminal, solitary or on short, 1.5cm stalks, small, 1cm, pale yellow-green or creamy petals with a purple-brown centre, sweet-scented. **Fruit:** Apr–Jul, distinctively pear-shaped, a smooth and woody brown capsule, 4–6cm, with pale warts, splitting in half and shedding 4 winged seeds. **Notes:** Leaves browsed by herbivores. Extracts of leaves and roots used to treat eye ailments. **Other species:** 1 in Zambia: *S. alata* occurs as a tall tree, mainly in northern mist-belt evergreen forest, with imparipinnate leaves, 5–7 leaflets and narrower fruit.

BEST SEEN
North and South Luangwa, Lower Zambezi and Kafue, and medium-altitude woodland

Afrocanthium lactescens Large-leaved Canthium

LOCAL NAMES: **Munkolobondo, Mfungo**

A small, unarmed deciduous tree, H 6m, S 3–4m, with distinctive horizontal branches and large paired leaves, which turn yellow in autumn. In low densities at medium altitudes, mainly on sandy and rocky soils, commonly in Munga and Kalahari woodland, occasionally in Miombo and Chipya woodland. **Bark:** Grey, smooth, becoming darker, purplish and rough. Bark and leaves exude a light amber gum when damaged. **Leaves:** End of lateral branchlets, simple, opposite, paired, 12 x 8cm, ovate to broadly elliptic, green, soft and leathery, sometimes velvety below, with veins prominent and sometimes hairy, base rounded and

apex tapering abruptly. Petiole 1–1.5cm. A pair of leaves and internode added annually. **Flowers:** Sep–Feb, in profuse, multi-flowered heads, small, white to pale yellow-green and sweetly scented. **Fruit:** Apr–Jul, asymmetrically round to squarish, 2-lobed berry, 7–11mm, green becoming brown or purple. **Notes:** Edible fruit. Host plant for Banded Monkey Moth *Jana eurymas*. **Other species:** 4 in Zambia: *A. pseudorandii* has smaller leaves, at low altitudes on rocky slopes, in jesse thicket or Kalahari Sand.

BEST SEEN
North, central and southern national parks and plateau woodland

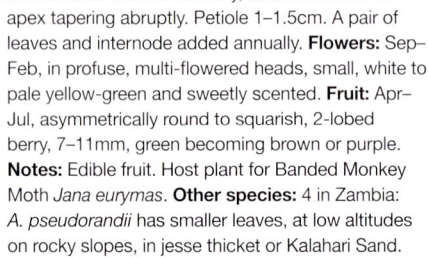

Breonadia salicina Adina

A medium-sized to large evergreen tree, H 40m, S 8–15m, with branches growing upwards and then drooping laterally. Locally common in low-altitude riverine vegetation across the east and centre, on sandy and rocky soils. **Bark:** Dark brown and rough, with vertical ridges. **Leaves:** Clustered at the end of branches, simple, in whorls of 4, or alternate, lanceolate or thinly elliptic, 10 x 5cm, glossy dark green above, paler below, leathery and hairless, tapering at both ends, veins conspicuously yellow-green. Petiole thick, 2cm. **Flowers:** Dec–Mar, on compact axillary balls, < 4cm, very small, inconspicuous, pale yellow-green or mauve, sweetly scented, with prominent stamens and supporting stalks, < 6cm. **Fruit:** Jun–Jul, a 2-lobed warty capsule-ball, 2–3mm, dark brown, containing numerous small seeds winged at both ends. **Notes:** Timber is light brown, oily and distinctively scented, prized. Bark has medicinal properties. **Other species:** A single-species genus across all of tropical Africa and Madagascar. **Protected in South Africa.**

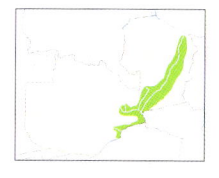

BEST SEEN
Rivers in northern, eastern and southern national parks

Canthium glaucum Pink-fruited Canthium

IN ZAMBIA SUBSP. *FRANGULA*: a semi-evergreen, multi-branched tree, H 5m, S 3–4m, with long, drooping branches and opposite pairs of straight, 2cm-long spines. Confined to the south and west at low altitudes, mainly on sandy and clay soils, common in Miombo and Kalahari woodland, and jesse and riverine thicket, occasionally on termite mounds and rocky outcrops. **Bark:** Grey to brown with white lenticels on branches. **Leaves:** In clusters on dwarf spurs near spine nodes, simple, ovate-elliptic, 4 x 2cm, green and hairless above, paler below, leathery, sometimes hairy, with base and apex both slightly tapering. Petiole

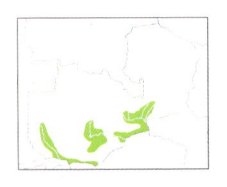

1–1.5cm. **Flowers:** Nov–Jan, in axillary, 2–8-flowered clusters on long stems, very small, whitish to greenish, scentless. **Fruit:** Feb–Mar, a smooth capsule on a long stem, 2.5–6cm, ovoid to pear-shaped, 0.9–1.2cm, green, ripening to pink or red. **Notes:** Astringent fruit edible. **Other species:** Only this species in Zambia, with 3 subspecies. A poorly defined genus with > 100 species in tropical Africa, Madagascar and Asia.

BEST SEEN
Central, southern and western national parks and low-altitude thickets

Feretia aeruginescens Pink Medlar

A small deciduous, sometimes scrambling tree, H 4m, S 3m, branching upwards, with branchlets opposite and hairy. Occurring locally at lower altitudes in riverine vegetation and *Combretum* thicket, mainly on sandier soils near water, springs or pans, not in the northwest. **Bark:** Brown or grey-brown top layer with reddish scales and both vertical and horizontal fissures, flaking in circular patches. **Leaves:** On short branchlets, simple, opposite, obovate to oblanceolate, 7 x 3cm, glossy dark green above, and reddish-brown and hairy below with prominent parallel veins, leathery, with tapering base, and the apex tapering and sharply tipped. Petiole short, 1–3mm. **Flowers:** Oct–Nov, attractive, solitary or in clusters on the branchlets, 1.5cm, white flushed with pink. **Fruit:** Jun–Sep, round, 1.5cm, pink becoming scarlet when ripe, usually retaining the calyx. **Notes:** Fruit eaten by birds and small mammals. An attractive garden plant. **Other species:** None in Zambia; 1 other species in tropical Africa.

> **BEST SEEN**
> Most national parks, but unobtrusive

Gardenia imperialis Large Pink Gardenia

LOCAL NAMES: Munamba, Utoto

IN ZAMBIA SUBSP. *IMPERIALIS*: a small and slender semi-evergreen tree, H 12m, S 6m, with spreading branches and a rounded crown. Frequent in the north in riparian forest, wet dambos and swamp forest, scarcer in the drier east and southwest. **Bark:** Pale grey, smooth becoming dark brown, with papery scales and horizontal rings. **Leaves:** At the end of branchlets, simple and opposite or in whorls, elliptic to obovate, 15 x 7cm, glossy dark green above, paler below, sometimes with soft hairs, leathery, heavily veined, base tapering to rounded and apex sharply tapering. Petiole thick, 2cm. **Flowers:** Aug–Feb, on axillary

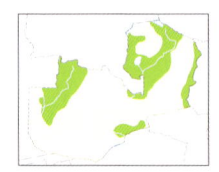

stalks, large and tubular, 13cm, petals creamy-white with pink, green or red tinge, waxy and sweet-scented. **Fruit:** Nov onwards, egg-shaped, 5–6cm, green becoming yellow, smooth, with remains of the flower retained at the apex. **Notes:** Leaves believed to have supernatural and medicinal properties. **Other species:** 5 other species and 2 varieties in Zambia, either with distinctly hairy leaves or on termite mounds. *G. ternifolia* is possibly the most widespread. *Rothmannia* species are similar but have lanceolate leaves, smaller flowers and often with no persistent calyx on the fruit.

BEST SEEN
Northern national parks, and southern and western streamlines

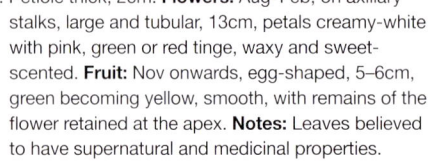

Vangueriopsis lanciflora False Wild Medlar

LOCAL NAMES: **Mufilu, Mufumu, Muhole, Mushambashamba, Maula-ula**

A small semi-deciduous tree, H 12m, S 5–9m, with a straight stem, branching stiffly upwards and laterally, then drooping, branchlets not velvety. Widespread but occasional, on sandy and rocky soils, commonly in Kalahari and escarpment Miombo woodland, infrequent in other woodland types, but not Mopane. **Bark:** Rusty-red, powdery, ageing to grey-brown, with local flaking revealing reddish under-bark. **Leaves:** Simple, opposite, oblong to oblanceolate, thin, large, 16 x 6cm, dull green and rough above, yellowish and hairy below, with prominent veins, leathery, margin entire and wavy, with base and apex rounded to slightly tapering. Petiole thick, 1cm. **Flowers:** Jul–Oct, at nodes of leafless branchlets, from branched, horn-shaped, hairy leaf buds, 2.5cm, with creamy-white curled-back petals, sweet-smelling. **Fruit:** May–Jun, a woody capsule, asymmetrically round, 2.5cm, smooth to slightly hairy, with 2 valves, each with 1 wrinkled grey seed. **Notes:** Bark and roots have medicinal properties. Flowers attract bees. Fruit is edible but flesh is acidic. Truncheons are used to make living fences. **Other species:** 3 in tropical Africa. *Vangueria infausta* is similar, but has hairy branchlets and elliptic or round leaves.

BEST SEEN
Most national parks in sandy and rocky areas

Anisophyllea boehmii **Mufungo**

An untidy-looking, medium-sized evergreen or semi-evergreen tree, H 10m, S 6–8m, with erect branches and a rounded crown. Occurs widely across the northern, high-rainfall belt in Miombo, Chipya and *Cryptosepalum* woodland. **Bark:** Red-brown, becoming grey-brown, rough and irregularly cracked. **Leaves:** Simple, alternate, 6 x 2.5cm, darkish green, leathery and hairy, distinctively only 2 pairs of almost parallel lateral veins either side of the midrib. **Flowers:** Apr–Dec, on woolly stalks, 8–9cm, small, 2–3cm, showy white or pink. **Fruit:** Jul–Mar, a round, fleshy drupe, 2.5cm, red becoming

purplish, with a single seed. **Notes:** Edible fruit is pleasant-tasting and potentially valuable, but fruiting is erratic; also favoured by mammals and birds. Roots are reported to be used against snakebite. **Other species:** 1 other species in Zambia: *A. quangensis* is a low-growing shrub.

BEST SEEN
Northern and northwestern national parks, and Miombo woodland

Cussonia arborea **Cabbage Tree**

A small, distinctive deciduous tree, H 13m, S 6–8m, with a short stem branching to separate crowns. Branchlets are often covered in hardened gum. A widespread tree of Miombo woodland, but only occurs occasionally, at low and medium altitudes, often in rocky areas and escarpments, also sometimes in Munga and Chipya woodland; not in the southwest. **Bark:** Grey to grey-brown, corky, deeply fissured, ridged and scaly. Exudes a clear gum when damaged. **Leaves:** Crowded at branch ends, palmate, divided into 7–9 usually toothed leaflets, large, 20 x 10cm, blue-green, thin and leathery. Petiole long, 50cm. Leafless Jun–Oct. **Flowers:** Aug–Nov, on distinctive, long, thin spikes, < 50cm, in terminal groups of 10 to 12, stalkless, creamy-green to yellowish. **Fruit:** Jan–Mar, clustered on hanging spikes, very small, 4–5mm, purple-black. **Notes:** Wood is soft and white, used for utensils, soft carvings and marimba (xylophone) keys. Bark has medicinal properties. Fruit is edible and hosts an edible caterpillar. **Other species:** 2 in Zambia: *C. spicata* is similar, but with 5 digitate leaflets and thick flowering stems; *C. corbisieri* is a suffrutex.

BEST SEEN
Escarpment Miombo, Nsumbu, North and South Luangwa, Lower Zambezi and Kafue

Cordia africana Large-leaved Cordia

LOCAL NAME: Muyotamfumu

A medium-sized deciduous or semi-deciduous tree, H 15m, S 4–8m, with spreading branches and a round crown. Widespread at low and medium altitudes, particularly in moist alluvial or riparian communities, also in Munga and Lake Basin Chipya woodland. **Bark:** Light brown becoming dark brown, smoothish but striated. **Leaves:** Simple, alternate, sometimes opposite, ovate, large, 13 x 9cm, green, paler below, leathery, with 5–7 pairs of lateral veins and margin entire. Petiole grooved, < 15cm. **Flowers:** Apr–Jun, in dense terminal heads, sweet-smelling trumpets, 2–3cm, showy white. **Fruit:** Jul–Oct, a leathery-

skinned drupe, 10cm, with persistent calyx at the base. Flesh mucilaginous, yellow to orange, sweet and edible. **Notes:** Wood light brown, polishes well. Used as shade trees in coffee plantations. Reasonably easy to propagate, a frost-tender garden tree, with fallen flowers creating a white carpet. Fruit is edible. **Other species:** 5 in Zambia, mostly scrambling shrubs: *C. goetzei* has waxier leaves; *C. pilossisima* has furry leaves; *C. sinensis* has small, leathery leaves and occurs in the south.

Trema orientale **Pigeonwood**

A semi-evergreen shrub or tree, H 18m, S 20m, with spreading branches giving dappled shade. Occurs in low densities, usually in riverine or montane habitats on sandy and alluvial soils, but not on Kalahari Sand. Often a pioneer tree in disturbed areas. **Bark:** Grey or creamy-brown and smooth, but with parallel marks. **Leaves:** Simple, alternate, ovate to lanceolate, 14 x 4cm, light green, papery, 3-veined from the rounded base, hairless above, paler below, with veins prominent and sometimes hairy, apex tapering sharply, margin finely serrated. Petiole short, 5–10mm. **Flowers:** Mainly Dec–Feb, but seen year-round, in dense axillary cymes, small, inconspicuous, green or yellow-green. Mostly male flowers, with fewer female flowers above or separate. **Fruit:** Jan–Jun, clustered on short axillary stalks, a glossy berry, 4–6mm, black, with a single black seed in bright green flesh. Fruit ripens on the tree. **Notes:** Birds favour the fruit. Bark and leaves have medicinal properties and produce dark-coloured dyes. Germinates readily and is fast-growing. A good garden or avenue tree. **Other species:** Only a single species in Africa.

BEST SEEN
Disturbed areas and low densities in most eastern national parks

Parinari curatellifolia Mubula Plum

LOCAL NAMES: Mupundu, Mubula, Mucha, Mpundu, Mula

A medium-sized to large evergreen tree, H 20m, S 6–12m, with a single trunk and spreading, dense crown; . Widespread, common on sandy soils in plateau Miombo, Chipya and Kalahari woodland. **Bark:** Grey-brown becoming dark, rough, with fairly uniform scales. Exudes red sap when damaged. **Leaves:** Simple, alternate or spirally arranged, elliptic, 7 x 3cm, dark green above, greyer and hairy below, margins entire and sometimes wavy. Numerous parallel lateral veins. **Flowers:** Jul–Oct, in branching heads, small, white to pinkish, sweet-scented. **Fruit:** May–Nov, an elongated, leathery-skinned, fleshy

drupe, 2–5cm, around a hard stone with a single seed. **Notes:** Wood used for canoes and mortars. Leaves and bark yield a red dye. Fruit edible, high in vitamin C, makes a good drink; the stone is rich in oils. Leaves, fruit and deep shade are favoured by wildlife. Often community-protected. An mpundu tree marks the site where David Livingstone died. **Other species:** 2 in Zambia: *P. capensis* is a shrub in drier areas; similar *P. excelsa* is a large tree with tapering pointy leaflets, found in the north.

BEST SEEN

Woodlands on the plateau and lower altitudes, also most national parks

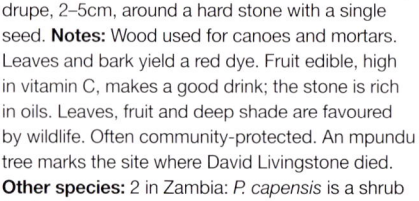

Marquesia macroura **Museshi**

LOCAL NAMES: **Museshi, Musanya, Mufuka**

A tall evergreen tree, H 25m, S 8–10m, with a buttressed, sometimes-flattened trunk and a spreading crown. Occurs across the northern, high-rainfall belt in dry evergreen, Miombo, Chipya and Kalahari woodland, often locally dominant. **Bark:** Grey-brown, rough and flaked. **Leaves:** Simple, alternate, ovate-lanceolate, 8 x 3.5cm, glossy green above, grey-green below, papery, with margins entire. Petiole conspicuous. **Flowers:** Jun–Oct, on terminal sprays, 2–9cm, small, 8mm, pink-creamy and fragrant. **Fruit:** Sep–Nov, a small, 5-winged, ovoid fruit, 0.5cm, pale green or straw-coloured, with a single brown seed. **Notes:** A relict species of previous wetter climates, probably more widespread in the past. Wood is difficult to work, but good for fence poles and charcoal. A good bee tree, the bark is used for traditional hives. Fungal associations include several chanterelle species (*chitondo*). **Other species:** 1 other species in Zambia: similar *M. acuminata* is taller (35m), has broader ovate leaves, white flowers, and is confined to dry evergreen forest.

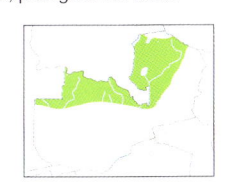

BEST SEEN
Evergreen forest and northern national parks

Monotes glaber Yellow-fruited Monotes

LOCAL NAMES: **Chimpampa, Mutembo, Kanyelele, Mkalakate**

A small to medium-sized semi-deciduous tree, H 12m, S 4–6m, with upward-spreading branches and a moderately dense crown; usually monoecious. Occurs on sandy soils in the west and south, frequently in dambo margins and on Kalahari Sand, also occasionally in Miombo and Munga woodland. **Bark:** Grey to grey-brown, irregularly fissured and ribbed, with rectangular scales. **Leaves:** Simple, alternate, oblong to elliptical, 7 x 3cm, shiny yellow-green above, dull green below, leathery, with 8–11 pairs of parallel lateral veins extending almost to the margin. Petiole < 1.5cm. **Flowers:** Nov–Apr, in

axillary heads, star-shaped, 1–1.5cm, greenish-yellow. **Fruit:** Feb–Aug, a round, ridged capsule, 10mm, yellow-brown, with persistent straw-coloured sepals. **Notes:** Wood is reddish-brown and brittle, but polishes well. Bark and leaves have some medicinal properties. All *Monotes* species are good 'bee trees', yielding high-quality honey from the nectar. The edible caterpillar *Usta terpsichore* (*finachimpampa*) is associated with several *Monotes* species. **Other species:** 11 in Zambia, often with limited distributions or habitat-specific, needing detailed reference material for accurate identification.

> **BEST SEEN**
> Central, southern and western national parks

Monotes katangensis Red-fruited Monotes

A small to medium-sized deciduous tree, H 15m, S 6–8m, with a spreading crown, sometimes also with a swollen trunk; usually monoecious. Widespread, but notably absent from the southwest as far north as Mongu. Most frequently in dambo margins and in plateau and escarpment Miombo and Lake Basin Chipya, also in Munga and Kalahari woodland. **Bark:** Grey to grey-brown, irregularly fissured, with rectangular scales. **Leaves:** Simple, alternate, oblong to elliptical, 8 x 5cm, light green with a yellowish, hairy, lower surface, thick, leathery and brittle, with parallel lateral veins extending to the margin. Petiole < 1.5cm. **Flowers:** Apr–Oct, conspicuous in velvety terminal bunches, creamy to greenish-yellow.

Fruit: Feb–Aug, a round capsule, 7mm, brown, with 5 showy, crimson, net-veined wings. **Notes:** Wood is reddish-brown and brittle but polishes well. Bark and leaves have some medicinal properties. All *Monotes* species are good 'bee trees' producing high-quality honey from the nectar. The edible caterpillar *Usta terpsichore* (*finachimpampa*) is associated with several *Monotes* species. A good garden specimen tree. **Other species:** 11 in Zambia, often with limited distributions or habitat-specific, needing detailed reference material for identification.

BEST SEEN
Woodland areas
and most
national parks

Diospyros kirkii Large-seed Jackal Berry

LOCAL NAMES: Mukolofuma, Mukyengya, Muchenjelekete, Mkulo, Muchenje

A medium-sized evergreen or semi-evergreen tree, H 11m, S 6–8m, with spreading branches and an open crown; dioecious. Widespread except in the southwest, most common in escarpment Miombo and Mopane woodland. **Bark:** Dark brown becoming black, fissured and scaly. **Leaves:** Simple, spirally arranged, large and thick, rounded, 12 x 7cm, dull green, hairy, velvety and brittle, with 6–8 pairs of subparallel lateral veins, becoming thicker towards the midrib. **Flowers:** Sep–Dec, small, creamy to pinkish, hairy and fragrant. **Fruit:** Jul–Oct, a fleshy round drupe, 3.5cm,

yellow-green to orange, containing 4 brown seeds. **Notes:** Fruit is edible with a refreshing sweet and floury taste. Cultivation for fruit has been suggested. A good shade tree. **Other species:** 16 other species and varieties in Zambia, adapted to both high- and low-rainfall areas, some are low-growing shrubs. *D. kirkii* is larger than all other *Diospyros* species in Zambia except *D. mespiliformis*, with which it can hybridise.

BEST SEEN
Woodland and most national parks except Sioma Ngwezi and Liuwa Plain

Diospyros mespiliformis **Jackal Berry**

A tall evergreen or semi-evergreen tree, H 26m, S 10–15m, sometimes buttressed, with rounded crown; dioecious. New branchlets covered in fine hairs. Widespread in riparian and lagoon habitats, and in wetter areas on termitaria. **Bark:** Brownish, darkening with age, becoming grey-brown, rough and fissured. May exude a dark gum when damaged. **Leaves:** Simple, alternate, oblong to elliptical, 9 x 3cm, dark glossy green above, paler below, leathery. New leaves pink. **Flowers:** Sep–Dec, 1cm, creamy to yellow, with hairs, fragrant. **Fruit:** Apr–Sep, round, fleshy, 2.5cm, yellow-green, holding 3–6 glossy dark brown seeds. **Notes:** Wood pinkish to grey, hard, heavy, mostly termite-resistant, workable, can produce a fine finish. Fruit is edible, relished by elephants, most antelope, jackals, baboons, monkeys and frugivorous birds; also has antibiotic properties and is widely used for skin and fertility treatment. **Other species:** 16 other species and varieties in Zambia, adapted to high and low rainfall. Similar to *D. kirkii*, also to *Mimusops zeyheri*.

BEST SEEN
Most national parks

Adansonia digitata Baobab

LOCAL NAMES: **Mubuyu, Muyu, Mkulukumba, Mlambe**

A majestic deciduous tree, H < 20m, S 6–12m, with a characteristic bulbous trunk, tapering branches and rounded crown. Those exceeding a 10m girth may be over 2,000 years old. Common in low-altitude Kalahari, Mopane and Munga woodland. **Bark:** Pinkish, smooth, becoming grey and wrinkled. Exudes gum when damaged. **Leaves:** Clustered at branch ends, simple initially, then trifoliate becoming digitate, with 3–9 dark green elliptical leaflets, 10 x 5cm. Leafless May–Nov. **Flowers:** Oct–Jan, large spherical buds on long stalks, opening with the new leaves as showy, 20cm flowers, white, smelling of

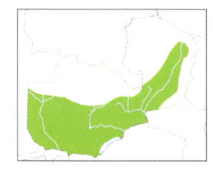

carrion. **Fruit:** Apr–May, an oval capsule, 12 x 6cm, grey-green becoming yellow-brown, woody, hairy, indehiscent, containing up to 100 kidney-shaped seeds in edible, ascorbic pulp. **Notes:** Flowers and hollow stems attract bats, flowers also attract various flies. Fruit, a source of ascorbic acid and vitamin C, is eaten by birds and other wild animals. Fibrous inner bark is used for making rope and mats. Grows well in gardens but needs space. **Other species:** One species in Africa.

> **BEST SEEN**
> All valley
> national parks

Thespesia garckeana Tree Hibiscus

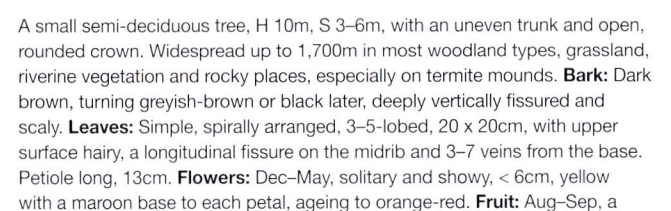

A small semi-deciduous tree, H 10m, S 3–6m, with an uneven trunk and open, rounded crown. Widespread up to 1,700m in most woodland types, grassland, riverine vegetation and rocky places, especially on termite mounds. **Bark:** Dark brown, turning greyish-brown or black later, deeply vertically fissured and scaly. **Leaves:** Simple, spirally arranged, 3–5-lobed, 20 x 20cm, with upper surface hairy, a longitudinal fissure on the midrib and 3–7 veins from the base. Petiole long, 13cm. **Flowers:** Dec–May, solitary and showy, < 6cm, yellow with a maroon base to each petal, ageing to orange-red. **Fruit:** Aug–Sep, a round capsule, yellow and woody, divided into five sections, with hairy lobes splitting to show edible, sweet brown flesh containing 15–30 pale brown seeds. Staying on the tree. **Notes:** Makes good firewood, also a source of bow wood and timber for small furniture. A garden shade tree with a non-aggressive root system. Browsed by wildlife, also a food plant for several moth and butterfly species. **Other species:** None in Zambia, a single-species genus in Africa.

BEST SEEN
In low densities in most national parks

Dombeya rotundifolia **Wild Pear**

LOCAL NAMES: Mukole, Chinga, Mulenshya, Mchiu, Mutobo

A small deciduous tree, H 14m, S 3–8m, often multi-stemmed, with an upright habit. Unmistakable in flower. Widespread in most woodland types, but not in the west, most common in plateau Miombo. **Bark:** Reddish-brown ageing to greyish-black, rough and fissured. **Leaves:** Simple, alternate, almost round, 15 x 15cm, grey-green, leathery and roughly hairy, with 3–7 veins from the base. Petiole < 8cm. Leafless from July to after flowering. **Flowers:** Jul–Oct, in axillary, branched heads, sweet-smelling and showy, 1.5–2cm, petals white or pale pink, becoming brown and remaining, forming dispersal wings for

the fruit. **Fruit:** Oct–Dec, round, 6mm, pale brown or cream with silky hairs. Holding up to 3 small brown seeds. **Notes:** Young bark is used for rope-making. Preparations of bark and roots used to relieve constipation. A good bee tree from Jul–Sep when in flower. A spectacular garden specimen or avenue tree. **Other species:** 6 other species in Zambia, all with attractive flowers: *D. burgessiae* and *D. wittei* are shrubs with showy pink flowers, *D. kirkii* is a low-altitude riverine thicket tree with small, white flowers.

BEST SEEN
Plateau Miombo
and most national
parks, except in
the southwest

Sterculia africana False Baobab

A medium-sized, stout, deciduous tree, H 12m, S 6–10m, branches often upward-curving from the nodes. In rocky escarpments, dry thicket, and on limestone outcrops and termite mounds at low to medium altitudes, except in Luapula Province and the southwest. **Bark:** Whitish with reddish coating, smooth, peeling to reveal cream under-bark. **Leaves:** Clustered at branch ends, digitate, circular to 3–5-lobed, 9 x 7cm, olive-green and furry, 7-veined from the base. Petiole long, 10cm. Leafless Jul–Nov. **Flowers:** Aug–Nov, before the new leaves, in terminal panicles, 9cm, compact, 2.5cm, greenish-yellow with red veining. **Fruit:** Apr–Jul, boat-shaped beaked capsules, 15cm, golden-velvet and woody, with intensely irritant hairs. Fruit splits on one side to release several blue-black seeds; favoured by *Dysdercus* beetles. **Notes:** Bark is used for nets and mats. Seeds are favoured by hornbills. Yields a brown tragacanth-like gum. **Other species:** 4 in Zambia: *S. mhosya*, *S. subviolacea* and *S. tragacantha* are northern lakeside or riverine forest species. *S. quinqueloba* is a distinctly tall escarpment tree.

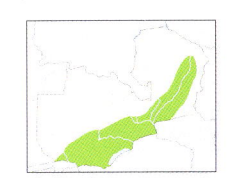

BEST SEEN
Eastern and southern valley national parks

Sterculia quinqueloba Large-leaved Star Chestnut

A large deciduous tree, H 20m, S 10–15m, with a straight white trunk; branches spread straight from nodes; dioecious. Common in low- to medium-altitude rocky escarpments in many woodland types except in the southwest; occasionally on termite mounds. **Bark:** Changing from greenish with a reddish coating to characteristic pale cream or purple, smooth and peeling in flakes. Produces brown gum when damaged. **Leaves:** Clustered at branch ends, digitate, 3–5-lobed, large, 25 x 25cm, bright green above, grey and hairy below, drying to yellow. Leafless May–Nov. **Flowers:** Feb–Jun, inconspicuous, on long

stalks, yellowish and foul-smelling. **Fruit:** Jun–Oct, a lobed follicle, 2–3cm, with irritant hairs, each with 2 or 3 black seeds; often eaten on the ground by *Dysdercus* beetles. **Notes:** Wood is light, logged and planked for timber. Bark and leaves have medicinal uses. Inner bark used for nets and mats. A spectacular garden tree; used for avenues, where the new and drying leaves are eye-catching. **Other species:** 4 in Zambia: *S. mhosya*, *S. subviolacea* and *S. tragacantha* are northern lakeside or riverine forest species with unilobed leaves; *S. africana* is usually multi-stemmed, with larger seed pods.

> **BEST SEEN**
> Rift valley
> escarpments and
> national parks, and
> Lochinvar and Kafue

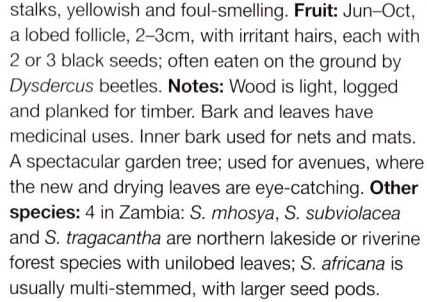

Ochna pulchra   Peeling-bark Ochna

LOCAL NAMES: Kabanga, Musengu, Kashushu, Munyelenyele, Mukanga

A small semi-deciduous tree, H 12m, S 5–8m, multi-branched with an untidy crown. Widespread on sandy soils in Miombo and Chipya woodland, dambo margins, and occasionally in *Cryptosepalum*, *Baikiaea* and Mopane woodland. **Bark:** Distinctive, creamy-white, becoming grey-brown and notably rough and scaly on the lower stem, flaking and smooth above. **Leaves:** Simple, whorled to alternate, elliptic to oblanceolate, 7.5 x 3cm, bright, glossy yellow-green above and paler below, tapering to the base and the apex, minutely toothed. Petiole stout and short, 6mm. **Flowers:** Aug–Nov, showy, on slender stalks in short-lived terminal racemes, 2cm, pale yellow and sweet-scented. **Fruit:** Nov–Dec, borne on stalks in clusters of up to 4, with bright red persistent sepals, a kidney-shaped, spectacularly glossy drupe, 1.5cm, containing a single seed. **Notes:** Attracts bees. Fruit eaten by monkeys and birds. Produces a bad-smelling oil; the smell is lost when it is made into soap. **Other species:** 18 species and 3 subspecies in Zambia, many are small shrubs: *O. schweinfurthiana* has particularly showy yellow flowers. A large genus in the Old World tropics.

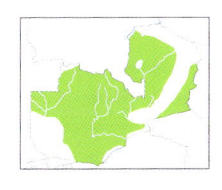

BEST SEEN
Most plateau national parks on sandy soils

Ochna schweinfurthiana Square-scaled Ochna

LOCAL NAMES: Iconi, Musengu, Mchoni, Patwe, Munyelenyele

A small semi-deciduous tree, H 7m, S 3–5m, upward branching with a rounded crown. Widespread on sandy soils in all woodland types. **Bark:** Dark grey-brown, cracked into uniform square scales with bark peeling into thin, papery strips. **Leaves:** Simple, whorled, opposite or alternate, elliptic, 8 x 4cm, light olive-green above and paler below, with base tapering, apex rounded, and margin bluntly toothed. Petiole stout, < 1.5cm. Young leaves coppery. **Flowers:** Sep–Nov, showy but short-lived, in short-stemmed, terminal bunches, < 1.5cm, bright yellow, sweet-scented. **Fruit:** Oct–Jan,

in short clusters of 2–4 drupes per stalk, with brick-red persistent sepals, each ovoid drupe 9mm, glossy black, containing a single seed. **Notes:** Attracts bees. Fruit eaten by monkeys and birds. **Other species:** 18 species and 3 subspecies in Zambia, many are small shrubs: *O. pulchra* does not have square-scaled bark or leaves with visibly toothed margins.

BEST SEEN
Plateau Miombo and most national parks with escarpments

Ximenia caffra Sour Plum

IN ZAMBIA VAR. *CAFFRA*: a semi-deciduous scrambler or small tree, H 6m, S 5–7m, branches spine-tipped. Widespread, mainly in *Acacia* and Munga woodland, wooded grassland, rocky areas and on termite mounds. **Bark:** Grey or dark grey, rough and scaly on older plants. **Leaves:** Simple, in spine axils or clustered on lateral spurs, oblong-elliptic, 6 x 2.5cm, bluish or grey-green, rounded at base and apex, densely hairy when young, hairless later. Petiole short, 10mm. **Flowers:** Sep–Dec, clustered in the spine axils or lateral shoots, 1 or 2 small flowers per stalk, with creamy-white petals. **Fruit:** Nov–Mar, a fleshy, thin-skinned drupe, 2.5cm, yellow to bright red when ripe, with bitter orange flesh and a single seed. **Notes:** Sandalwood-scented wood can be turned. Branches used for bows. Leaves and roots have medicinal properties. Fruit edible. Seeds contain toxic hydrocyanic acid. **Other species:** 1 in Zambia. *X. americana* is similar, but has oblong, upward-folded leaves and young leaves are hairless.

BEST SEEN
Inconspicuous, but in most national parks and low-altitude woodland

Bridelia micrantha Mitzeeri

LOCAL NAMES: Musabayembe, Musebe, Mukunku, Mumbuza, Mlebezi, Munyansa

A small to medium-sized semi-deciduous tree, H 15m, S 5–10m, young branches spiny, sometimes retained in older trees; dioecious. Widespread except in the southwest, occurring in evergreen forest, occasionally in Miombo and Munga woodland. **Bark:** Reddish-brown becoming grey or dark brown, finely fissured. **Leaves:** Simple, alternate, variable, elliptic to obovate, 8 x 6cm, glossy dark green, paler below, hairless, with the base and apex tapering. Petiole short, 10mm. Young leaves purple, old leaves bright orange and red before falling. **Flowers:** Sep–Dec, in tight clusters in the leaf axils, very small,

petals creamy-green to white. **Fruit:** Nov–Mar, a small round berry, 8mm, shiny black, with a single bluish seed in edible greenish flesh. **Notes:** Wood dark brown, workable and takes a fine polish. Fruit edible and favoured by birds, also good for making jam and dye. All parts used in traditional medicine. A fast-growing shade tree, with leaves providing colour in the spring and autumn. **Other species:** 4 in Zambia, with 3 varieties of *B. cathartica*, a knobbly scrambler. The other species either on Kalahari Sand or granite sites, or with obovate leaves.

BEST SEEN
National parks
across the north
and centre

Pseudolachnostylis maprouneifolia **Duiker Berry**

LOCAL NAMES: **Kudu Berry, Musangati, Musolo, Mukunyu, Kabalabala, Msolo**

IN ZAMBIA VAR. *MAPROUNEIFOLIA*: a medium-sized deciduous tree, H 15m, S 15m, with zigzag upward- and outward-spreading drooping branches, with a roundish crown; dioecious. Widespread at all altitudes, mainly in plateau Miombo and Munga woodland. **Bark:** Creamy-grey or grey-brown, smooth, becoming cracked with long scales. **Leaves:** Simple, alternate, ovate-elliptic, variable, 6 x 4cm, grey-green but paler below, sometimes hairy, with both base and apex rounded. Petiole 1cm. Autumn leaf fall combines yellow, orange and red. **Flowers:** Jul–Dec, small, inconspicuous, creamy-green; male flowers few, in 2–3cm axillary clusters; female flowers solitary.

Fruit: May–Oct, a round, slightly grooved capsule, 2.5cm, green, ripening to yellow on the ground, with three sections, each with 1 flat, oval seed.

Notes: Wood, pale cream, is usable. Leaves and fruit are browsed by elephants, antelope and birds; also used to make dye. All parts used in traditional medicine. A good bee tree. **Other species:** A single variable species in Africa, with 4 varieties recorded in the region: var. *africana* has similar leaves, but is distinguished by its corky bark and leaves tinged red.

BEST SEEN
Most plateau woodlands and national parks

Uapaca kirkiana Wild Loquat

LOCAL NAMES: **Musuku, Muhaka, Kabofa, Mpotopoto, Msuku**

IN ZAMBIA VAR. *KIRKIANA*: a small semi-evergreen tree, H 13m, S 15m, multi-branched with a variable crown; dioecious. Widespread on sandy and stony soils, except in the west. Mainly in plateau Miombo and dominant in secondary Miombo. **Bark:** Dark grey, vertically fissured, cracked and scaly. **Leaves:** Clustered at branch ends, simple, alternate or spirally arranged, large, ovate to obovate, saddle-shaped, < 17 x 11cm, dull green, paler and hairy below, brittle, with numerous parallel veins almost reaching the margin. Petiole thick, 2cm. **Flowers:** Jan–Apr, small, inconspicuous, greenish-yellow; male

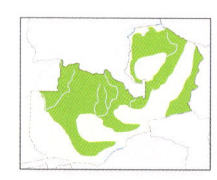

flowers in dense clusters along the stem; female flowers solitary. **Fruit:** Jul–Dec, a round fleshy drupe, 3–4cm, green ripening to rusty yellow, tough-skinned. The sweet, edible flesh contains 3–5 pale, ridged, pointed seeds. **Notes:** Wood reddish-brown, is usable. Fruit is edible and important in local nutrition, has significant commercial value; browsed by most ungulates and frugivorous birds. All parts used to treat indigestion. A good bee tree. **Other species:** 7 in Zambia and 3 varieties: all others occur in the centre and north. *U. robynsii* is similar, but veins curve forward near the margin.

BEST SEEN
Escarpment areas of rift valley parks and all plateau national parks

Uapaca nitida   **Narrow-leaved Uapaca**

IN ZAMBIA VAR. *NITIDA*: a small to medium-sized, semi-evergreen, upward-branching tree, H 12m, S 10m, with a dense, rounded crown; usually dioecious. Widespread in northern and central Zambia, at low and medium altitudes, on sandy and lateritic soils, mainly in plateau Miombo and Chipya woodland, but not in the west. **Bark:** Dark grey-black, very rough, vertically fissured and scaly. **Leaves:** Simple, alternate, ovate to obovate-elliptic, variable, 10 x 3.5cm, glossy green and leathery, tapering to the base, with up to 14 pairs of lateral veins looping before the margin. Petiole slender, 6cm. **Flowers:** Mar–May, small, inconspicuous, greenish-yellow; male flowers spread along the stem; female flowers solitary. **Fruit:** Jun–Sep, a round fleshy drupe, 2cm, green ripening to orange, tough-skinned. The sweet, edible flesh contains 3–5 pale, ridged, pointed seeds. **Notes:** Fruit is edible and important in local nutrition, but not of commercial value; browsed by most ungulates and frugivorous birds. In Tanzania, a decoction of the roots is used to treat malaria. **Other species:** 7 in Zambia and 3 varieties, all others occur in central and northern Zambia. *U. robynsii* is similar, but veins curve forward near the margin.

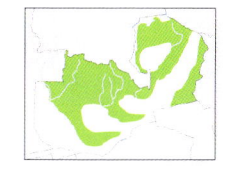

BEST SEEN
Northern and central plateau national parks and escarpment areas

Securidaca longepedunculata Violet Tree

LOCAL NAMES: Mupapi, Muchacha, Mutata, Kapapi, Mwinda, Mupuluka, Bwazi

A small to medium-sized semi-deciduous spiny shrub or small tree, H 10m, S < 15m, with a sometimes-flattened stem, spreading branches and untidy canopy. Widespread, particularly in Munga, Chipya and Kalahari woodland and dry evergreen forest. **Bark:** Grey-brown becoming paler with age, deeply fissured. **Leaves:** Simple, alternate or spirally arranged, clustered at spur branchlets, variable, narrowly elliptic or oblong, 3 x 2cm, dark olive-green and leathery, tapering to the base, and with apex rounded. Petiole short. **Flowers:** Sep–Nov, with the new leaves, in showy, dense, terminal and axillary

sprays, small, 10mm, pink to purple, and sweetly violet-scented. **Fruit:** May–Nov, a round, 1cm nut combined with a single-veined wing to form a hatchet-shape, < 4cm, dark crimson ripening to yellow and then pale brown. **Notes:** Bark used to make soap and twine. All parts used to treat STDs, chest infections and rheumatism. Roots contain toxic methyl salicylate (oil of wintergreen). Browsed by wildlife. A good bee tree, also a food plant for many butterflies. An attractive garden specimen. **Other species:** 1 other species in Zambia: *S. welwitschii* is a **Vulnerable** liana in northern forests. A large genus.

BEST SEEN
Low- to medium-altitude woodland and most national parks

Faurea saligna Willow Beechwood

A graceful semi-evergreen tree, H 20m, S 10m, often with a twisted stem, upward-reaching branches and a conical crown. Occurs in low densities in most woodland types, most common in Miombo, Kalahari and Chipya woodland, but not in the southwest. **Bark:** Grey, dark grey or black with deep vertical fissures and very prominent ridging. **Leaves:** Clustered and drooping at branch ends, simple, alternate, lanceolate, 9 x 1.5cm, light yellowish-green becoming red in autumn, leathery and hairless, with veins joining to form a long vein just within the margin. Tapering at both ends. Petiole pink, 2cm. **Flowers:** Mar–Aug, in slender, hairy terminal spikes, 12–15cm, greenish to creamy-white and sweet-scented. **Fruit:** Sep–Mar, on the flower spike, club-shaped nutlets, brown with long silky-yellow hairs. **Notes:** Wood pale yellow-red, produces a fine polished finish and a red dye. A good bee tree. **Other species:** 4 in Zambia: *F. rochetiana* is also widespread, but has more angular branching, longer and broader leaves, and dense flowering spikes. The other species occur commonly in riverine forest in the north. *Searsia lancea* is similar but its leaves are trifoliate.

BEST SEEN
Low densities in most woodlands and national parks

Protea angolensis   Northern Protea

LOCAL NAMES: Sugar Bush, Musoso, Mulemu, Chilemu, Mufwamebo, Msakata (generic)

IN ZAMBIA VAR. *DIVARICATA*: an upward-branching evergreen shrub or small tree, H 3m, S 2m. Occasional in Miombo and Kalahari woodland on sandy and rocky soils in the north, northwest, centre and south, sometimes in stands, scarce in other woodlands. **Bark:** Black, finely fissured and horizontally cracked. **Leaves:** Clustered at branch ends, simple, alternate, broad, oblanceolate to elliptic, 13 x 6cm, grey-green, leathery, hairless, tapering to the base, with midrib prominent, and margin entire and wavy. Petiole short and thick, 1cm. New leaves pinkish. **Flowers:** Apr–Jul, solitary and large, 10–18cm, pink or white, with white

silky hairs with pink tips. On a scaly stalk. **Fruit:** Aug–Oct, a densely hairy, 4-sided nut. **Notes:** Nectar syrup used to treat chest disorder, bark and roots for treating stomach complaints. An attractive garden tree, favoured by insects, hornbills and insect-eating birds. Fibrous roots are used in basketry. **Other species:** 16 other species or subspecies in Zambia: *P. gaguedi* leaves less hairy and flowerhead remains cup-shaped; *P. madiensis* has large hairless leaves and pink-tipped flower bracts; *P. rupestris* is tall with rosette-like, hairy leaves and flowerheads clustered in groups of 2–4. Several of Zambia's mountain proteas are **Threatened** or **Vulnerable**.

BEST SEEN
Northern, northwestern and central national parks in plateau and escarpment Miombo

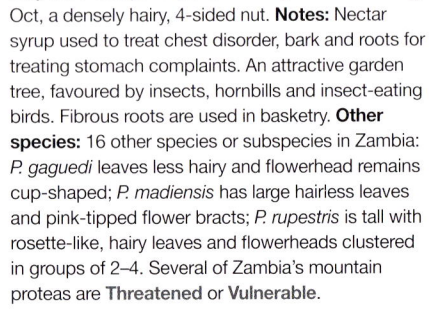

Protea gaguedi African Protea

A small, gnarled, evergreen multi-stemmed shrub or small tree, H 4–10m, S 2–3m, with upward-reaching branches and open crown. Common in central, southern and western Zambia. **Bark:** Grey to creamy or reddish-brown, corky, finely fissured, horizontally cracked. Young stems with orange-yellow hairs. **Leaves:** Clustered at branch ends, simple, alternate, oblong-elliptic to sickle-shaped, 13 x 2.5cm, light bluish-green, leathery, almost hairless, with prominent narrow yellow midrib. Margin tapers to base and tip. Petiole short and thick, 1cm. **Flowers:** Oct–Jun, on solitary, terminal stalks, conical, 4–10cm, white or pink-tinged, with 6 rows of silvery-haired bracts. Sweet-scented. **Fruit:** Sep–Oct, a hard, 1cm nutlet with dense golden hairs. Nutlet released from flowerhead as it dries and opens, leaving an empty flower cup. **Notes:** Most parts used in traditional medicine. Widespread in Africa; *gaguedi* is Ethiopian for protea. **Other species:** 16 other species or subspecies in Zambia: *P. angolensis* has hairy branchlets and broad, hairless leaves; *P. madiensis* has large hairless leaves and pink-tipped flower bracts; *P. rupestris* is tall with rosette-like, hairy leaves and flowerheads clustered in groups of 2–4. Several of Zambia's mountain proteas are **Threatened** or **Vulnerable**.

BEST SEEN

Rocky areas in most plateau national parks and plateau Miombo

Phyllogeiton discolor Bird Plum

LOCAL NAMES: Mutachi, Munzi, Makumba, Mwii, Mwinji, Munziyi, Nziyi

Usually a semi-deciduous tree, but sometimes a shrub, H 18m, S 8–12m, with branches growing upwards and then laterally. The crown is dense and umbrella-like. Confined to the drier east, south and west, and the shores of the northern lakes, but widely scattered. Often on termite mounds, in riverine forest or on sandier soils, occasionally in Mopane woodland. **Bark:** Dark grey or black, sometimes twisted, with deep vertical fissures separated into scales. **Leaves:** Simple, opposite, subopposite or alternate, elliptic to oblong-elliptic, 8 x 4cm, shiny green above and paler below, leathery, tapering

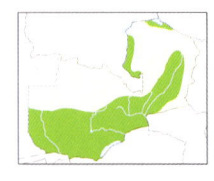

to the apex, base rounded, sometimes hairy on obvious herringbone veins. Petiole 1–1.5cm. **Flowers:** Oct–Feb, up to 10 on slender stalks in loose axillary clusters, small, greenish-yellow. **Fruit:** Feb–May, olive-like, edible, 2cm, yellow and smooth, containing 2 seeds, ripening on the tree. **Notes:** Wood yellow, one of the hardest timbers in Central Africa. Fruit is much-favoured and with a high vitamin C content. A good bee tree. **Other species:** None in Zambia. 11 others across Africa, East Asia and the west of North America.

BEST SEEN
Nsumbu, Luangwa, Lower Zambezi, Kafue and Sioma Ngwezi

Ziziphus mucronata **Buffalo Thorn**

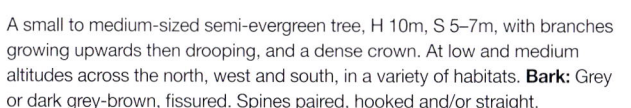

A small to medium-sized semi-evergreen tree, H 10m, S 5–7m, with branches growing upwards then drooping, and a dense crown. At low and medium altitudes across the north, west and south, in a variety of habitats. **Bark:** Grey or dark grey-brown, fissured. Spines paired, hooked and/or straight. **Leaves:** Simple, alternate, broadly ovate and markedly asymmetric, 5 x 3cm, shiny green above and slightly paler below, leathery, sometimes hairy, notably 3-veined from base, with apex tapering and apical margin finely toothed. Petiole short. **Flowers:** Oct–Mar, in tight axillary clusters, small, yellow, with copious nectar. **Fruit:** Mar–Aug, a spherical drupe, 1–1.5cm, ripening shiny red, with 2 glossy brown seeds in an edible pulp. Often staying on the tree. **Notes:** Leaves and bark used in a range of traditional medicines. Fruit is eaten by wild herbivores and birds, also a food plant for several species of butterfly and moth. A good bee tree. **Other species:** 3 in Zambia: *Z. abyssinica* is similar, widespread, with whole leaf margin toothed, veins depressed above, hairy below and larger fruit; *Z. mauritiana* is a naturalised exotic; *Z. pubescens* is thornless, only in Luangwa Valley.

> **BEST SEEN**
> Most national parks

Flacourtia indica   Governor's Plum

A semi-deciduous shrub or small tree, H 10m, S 3–5m, usually spiny, with crooked branches and a variable crown; dioecious. Widespread except in the northwest, at low to medium altitudes on sandier soils in most types of woodland. **Bark:** Pale grey and smooth, becoming dark brown or creamy-brown, with numerous white lenticels. Flaking reveals orange under-bark. Often armed with long, toxic spines, sometimes in branched masses on the trunk. **Leaves:** Simple, alternate, variably elliptic, ovate or round, 6 x 4cm, light to dark green above and below, leathery. Distinctively changing to red and purple in Sep. Base tapering and apex tapering to round, with margin entire or scalloped. Petiole 1.5cm. **Flowers:** Sep–Dec, in terminal or axillary sprays, < 2.5cm, small, 5mm, inconspicuous, greenish-yellow flushed with red, petals absent but stamens dense. **Fruit:** Jan–Jun, round and berry-like, ripening to red or purple, smooth, fleshy, with 4–8 chambers, each with a white seed in green, edible flesh. **Notes:** Leaves, bark and roots are used to treat fevers, diarrhoea and inflammation. Fruit is edible and refreshing, but acidic. Favoured by birds. **Other species:** Numerous other species in tropical Africa.

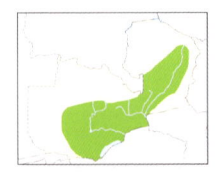

BEST SEEN
Most low- and medium-altitude national parks and woodland areas

Oncoba spinosa **Wild Rose**

A semi-deciduous spiny shrub or small tree, H 8m, S 3–6m, erect with drooping branches. Widespread and locally common, in riverine habitats and most woodland types on limestone soils and termite mounds, occasionally in Miombo woodland. Absent in the extreme north and southwest. **Bark:** Grey, smooth and mottled, sometimes scaly, with straight, 5cm-long spines. **Leaves:** Simple, alternate, ovate-elliptic, 6 x 3cm, glossy dark green above, less glossy below, base and apex tapering, and margin coarsely toothed. Petiole short. **Flowers:** Oct–Jan, solitary, axillary or terminal, large, < 9cm, with white petals with fried-egg-like central mass of golden stamens, sweet-scented. Individual flowers short-lived. **Fruit:** Apr–Jul, a round, indehiscent capsule, < 6cm, shiny green, ridged and woody, ripening red-brown, with numerous 6mm-long shiny brown seeds in edible, dry, yellow pulp. **Notes:** Wood light brown, gives a fine finish. Roots are used to treat intestinal and bladder complaints. Dried fruit used as snuff boxes and ankle rattles in traditional dancing. Seeds contain an oil used in paint. **Other species:** 3 in Zambia: *O. bukobensis* and *O. fragrans* confined to northern Zambia and 1 a subshrub in the west.

> ### BEST SEEN
> Most national parks, especially in riverine woodland

Balanites aegyptiaca Torchwood

LOCAL NAMES: Mubambwangoma, Mwalabwe, Nkuyu, Mulyanzovu

A small to medium-sized semi-evergreen tree, H 3–5m, S 3–4m, with a fluted trunk and spreading crown; dioecious. Branchlets have unbranched spines, < 7cm. Widespread in Mopane, Munga and Lake Basin Chipya woodland at low and medium altitudes, but seldom in the west. **Bark:** Creamy-brown to grey-brown, deeply fissured and scaly. Exudes a clear gum when damaged. **Leaves:** At spine or branchlet nodes, compound, paired, asymmetrically obovate, 4.5 x 3cm, grey-green, leathery. Petiole short. **Flowers:** Sep–Dec, in stalked bunches, 1.5–2cm, greenish-yellow to white. **Fruit:** Apr–Aug, an

elongated leathery capsule, 5 x 2.5cm, orange-red with odd-scented, oily-orange flesh covering a single, 5-angled stone in a fibrous coat. **Notes:** Leaves are high in protein; fruit is edible when ripe, but bitter – both are favoured by wildlife. Fruit makes a refreshing drink or alcoholic beverage. Seeds contain an oil used in cooking and cosmetics. Roots, wood and fruit contain a saponin used as a fish poison and bilharzia snail poison (1 fruit : 30 litres of water). Possible garden specimen tree. **Other species:** 1 other species in Zambia, 2 varieties of *B. aegyptiaca*. *B. maughamii* is a tall, buttressed tree with zigzagging branches and forked thorns.

BEST SEEN
Valley national parks except Sioma Ngwezi and Liuwa Plain

Colophospermum mopane **Mopane**

LOCAL NAMES: Mupane, Mwane, Mwaani, Chanye, Mpane

A large, deciduous tree, H 21m, S 6–10m, single-stemmed, with upward-spreading branches and a narrow crown. On heavy sodic clays in the main river valleys below 1,300m, sometimes in pure stands of gallery forest. Occasionally in other woodland types and on termite mounds. **Bark:** Grey becoming dark grey-brown, with deep vertical fissures and long, flaky scales. Produces a reddish gum when damaged. **Leaves:** Compound, bifoliate, resembling butterfly wings, 7 x 3cm, closing when hot, light glossy green, with several veins from the base. Petiole 2–4cm. Produce a turpentine smell when crushed. **Flowers:** Dec–Mar, in axillary sprays, greenish-yellow with reddish sepals.

Fruit: May–Oct, at branchlet ends, flat, kidney-shaped pods, 3–5cm, golden-brown. A single seed with attractive line pattern and numerous resin glands, germinates in the pod. **Notes:** Wood is heavy, straw-coloured, and polishes well. Leaves, bark and fruit are favoured by many species. Elephant browsing stunts large areas of mopane scrub. A larval food plant for Emperor Moth *Gonimbrasia belina*, producing popular edible mopane worms. **Other species:** A single species from Zambia to northern South Africa.

BEST SEEN
Luangwa, Lower Zambezi and Kafue valley national parks on heavy clay soils

Guibourtia coleosperma Zambian Rosewood

LOCAL NAMES: Mushibi, Muzauli

A large, almost-evergreen tree, H 25m, S 8–12m, usually with a tall, straight trunk, often buttressed or fluted, heavy, twisted, drooping lateral branches, and a dense, rounded crown. Confined to the west and southwest on Kalahari Sand, often codominant with *Cryptosepalum exfoliatum*. **Bark:** Characteristic grey and pinkish-cream, with flaking patches dark brown to black, giving a burnt look. **Leaves:** Alternate, compound, bifoliate, with a pair of opposite, sickle-shaped, asymmetrical leaflets, 6 x 3cm, glossy dark green above and paler below. Leaves larger at the base of the stem. **Flowers:** Nov–Mar, in showy clumps in terminal

heads, < 16cm, delicately star-shaped, 10mm, white. **Fruit:** May–Oct, a circular pod, 2–3cm, brown and woody, on a zigzag stalk, pod splitting and curling back one side to release a single shiny red-brown seed with scarlet aril, 10mm, attached by a thin thread. **Notes:** Wood pinkish to dark red-streaked and hard. Previously used for railway sleepers, but now a coveted exported hardwood timber. **Other species:** 1 other species in Zambia: *G. conjugata* has smaller, only slightly curved leaflets, and is confined to Zambezi Valley Mopane and deciduous thicket below Livingstone. **Vulnerable.**

BEST SEEN
Central and western national parks and associated Kalahari Sand habitats

Kigelia africana Sausage Tree

A medium-sized deciduous or semi-deciduous tree, H 25m, S 4–8m, with a single stem, spreading branches and a dense round crown. Distinctive when fruiting. At low and medium altitudes, in alluvial/riparian communities, less common in Munga and Lake Basin Chipya woodland. **Bark:** Light-brown becoming grey-brown, rough with patchy flakes. **Leaves:** Opposite or in whorls of 3, imparipinnate with 3–5 pairs of thick, oblong leaflets and a terminal leaflet, 8 x 6cm, yellowish-green, leathery and hairy, terminal largest. Petiole 15cm. **Flowers:** Aug–Nov, hanging on long stems, distinctive maroon-claret with yellow veining, borne in 6–12-flowered sprays. Flowers open at night and fall the next day, after pollination by bats, insects and wind. **Fruit:** Dec–Jun, a leathery-skinned sausage-shaped capsule, < 60cm, 10kg. Inner flesh soft and fibrous, with numerous flat brownish seeds. **Notes:** Flowers rich in nectar, favoured by bats, sunbirds and monkeys. Fallen flowers favoured by many herbivores. Fruit inedible for humans but eaten by hippo, rhino, squirrels and baboons. Extracts of bark and fruit have medicinal properties. Fruit extract used for skin upsets. **Other species:** A single-species genus in Africa.

BEST SEEN
All valley
national parks

Markhamia obtusifolia Golden Bell-bean

LOCAL NAMES: Musalankwale, Mutendankwale, Mukupukupu, Mususankwale

A small deciduous shrub or tree, H 12m, S 3–6m, with a spreading, open crown, and often with a crooked trunk. Young branchlets with golden hairs. Widespread at low to medium altitudes, except in montane forest and Itigi thicket. **Bark:** Pale brown becoming grey-brown, with characteristic striated vertical fissuring. **Leaves:** Opposite, compound, imparipinnate, with 3–5 pairs of thick, oblong to elliptic leaflets, 8 x 5cm, yellowish-green with dense golden hairs on the underside. Petiole 2–8cm long. **Flowers:** Jun–Nov, distinctive, solitary at leaf nodes, yellow with chocolate veining on the lower

3 corolla lobes, petals dropping within a few days. **Fruit:** May–Sep, a long, narrow, flat pod, < 85cm, orange-brown and hairy, splitting to release numerous flat, brown, winged seeds. **Notes:** Wood is heavy and strong. Twigs and bark are used for snaring francolin and spurfowl (*nkwale*), hence the local names. Bark makes a useful rope. *Markhamia* grows easily from seed or truncheons and makes a colourful garden specimen, but flowers for only a short period. **Other species:** 1 other species in Zambia: *M. zanzibarica* is similar, but with greener leaflets, maroon petals and a thicker, woodier pod.

BEST SEEN
Most woodland areas and national parks

Stereospermum kunthianum Pink Jacaranda

LOCAL NAMES: Kayubule, Mupafu, Mlakanjovu, Mtelelanjobvu, Kavunguti, Mutese

A small to medium-sized deciduous tree, H 13m, S 3–10m, with a single trunk, untidily spreading branches and an open crown; dioecious. Widespread as an occasional tree or in a stand in lower-rainfall areas at low and medium altitudes and on escarpments, often on termite mounds, in Munga and Lake Basin Chipya woodland. Not in the southwest. **Bark:** Distinctively grey and smooth, with flakes peeling off in patches. **Leaves:** Opposite, compound, imparipinnate, 2–4 pairs of stiff, oblong to elliptic leaflets, 7 x 3cm, green, underside hairy with prominent veins. Petiole 3–9cm. **Flowers:** Aug–Oct, large and showy in drooping sprays, bell-shaped, 1.5cm, pink. **Fruit:** Oct–Dec, a long, smooth, slender pod, 24–50cm, reddish-brown, splitting to release numerous winged seeds. Pod remains on the tree for months. **Notes:** Bark, roots, leaves and pods have medicinal properties. A spectacular garden specimen tree, especially when in flower. **Other species:** Only 1 other possible species in northern Zambia, currently being reviewed. 15 species in the Old World tropics.

BEST SEEN
Most national parks

Kirkia acuminata White Seringa

A medium-sized deciduous tree, H 21m, S 8–10m, with spreading branches and an open, rounded crown; dioecious. Confined to low and medium altitudes in the south, commonly in escarpment Miombo, but also Munga woodland and thicket. **Bark:** Grey-brown and smooth, vertically ridged. Inner bark is cream-coloured and corky. **Leaves:** At branch ends, alternate, compound, imparipinnate, 6–10 pairs of narrow, ovate leaflets, 5 x 1.5cm, with apex tapering and margin finely serrated. Young leaves sticky. **Flowers:** Oct–Jan, in loose branched axillary heads, < 7cm, small, creamy-green. **Fruit:** Apr–Aug,

sometimes later, a thin woody capsule, 1–2cm, brown, splitting into 4-winged sections joined at the apex, 1 seed in each. **Notes:** Wood light brown, takes a good polish, but is high in silica, blunting tools. Bark is used to make cloth. Roots store water, exploited by wildlife. **Other species:** None in Zambia. 4 species in tropical and southern Africa. *K. acuminata* is similar to *Sclerocarya birrea*, but the latter has a more spreading habit and no toothed edges to its broader leaflets.

BEST SEEN

Woodlands and Luangwa, Kafue and Zambezi valley national parks

Trichilia dregeana Forest Mahogany

A medium-sized to large evergreen tree, H 25m, S 8–15m, with a straight trunk, sometimes swollen or buttressed, and upward-spreading branches giving a dense, rounded crown. Occurring in the wetter north in evergreen and montane forest, and riparian woodland. **Bark:** Grey-brown and smooth. **Leaves:** Compound, imparipinnate, 3 or 4 pairs of opposite or alternate, obovate to oblong-elliptical leaflets, 21 x 8cm, glossy dark green above and paler below, leathery, with apex rounded. Petiole 8–10cm. **Flowers:** Sep–Nov, in short, branched axillary sprays, 5cm, large and creamy-white, petals, < 2.5cm, sweet-scented. **Fruit:** Dec–Mar, a round, wooden capsule without a distinct neck, 3cm, creamy-brown and velvety, splitting into 3 or 4 valves, revealing 3–6 glossy black seeds mostly surrounded by scarlet arils. **Notes:** Wood is reddish-brown, used in the timber trade. Seeds yield an oil used for soap. Most parts used in traditional medicine. Flowers and seeds attract several bird, butterfly and moth species. Good shade tree. **Other species:** 3 in Zambia, 2 are northern, understorey shrubs: *Khaya nyasica* is larger than *T. dregeana* and has paripinnate leaves. *T. emetica* smaller and widespread.

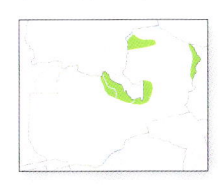

BEST SEEN
Northern plateau
national parks

Trichilia emetica Natal Mahogany

IN ZAMBIA SUBSP. *EMETICA*: a medium-sized to large evergreen shade tree, H 20m, S 8–10m, with a straight or multi-stemmed trunk, sometimes buttressed, upward-spreading branches, and a dense rounded crown. Widespread across the country at medium and low altitudes in evergreen forest, and riparian and Munga woodland. Infrequent in Kalahari Sand in the west. **Bark:** Grey-brown or brown, smooth or locally rough. **Leaves:** Compound, imparipinnate, with 4 or 5 pairs of opposite or subopposite oblong to elliptical leaflets, 12 x 5.5cm, dark glossy green above and densely hairy below, leathery, with apex rounded.

Petiole 7–12cm. **Flowers:** Aug–Oct, in short axillary heads, 5cm, small, 1.5cm, greenish-white, sweet-scented. **Fruit:** Dec–Mar, a wooden capsule, 2.5–3cm, with a distinct neck, creamy or reddish, velvety, splitting into 3 or 4 valves, with 3–6 glossy black seeds with scarlet arils. **Notes:** Widely planted garden and street tree with usable timber. Seeds yield a usable oil; most parts used medicinally. Flowers and seeds attract birds and insects. Leaves reported to soothe skin irritation from the Buffalo Bean *Mucuna coriacea*. **Other species:** 3 in Zambia: *T. dregeana* is larger, confined to northern forests, 2 are northern, understorey shrubs.

BEST SEEN
Riverine areas of most national parks, but less common in the west

Afzelia quanzensis Pod Mahogany

A large semi-deciduous tree, H 25m, S 8–12m, with a short, cylindrical, sometimes divided trunk, upward-spreading lateral branches, and a dense canopy. Widespread except in montane, dry evergreen and swamp forest areas. Especially abundant in Lake Basin Chipya and Kalahari woodland. **Bark:** Grey-brown, darkening over time, with large flakes cracking off leaving pale patches. **Leaves:** Compound, paripinnate, alternate, with 4–6 pairs of opposite or subopposite oblong-elliptic leaflets, 5 x 3cm, glossy green above and paler below. Petiole 2–6cm. Leafless Jul–Nov. **Flowers:** Jul–Nov, in sprays, 2–5cm, with a single red or pink petal, sweet-smelling. **Fruit:** Jun–Nov, a large, flattened, oblong wooden pod, 10–17cm, dark brown, splitting on the tree and releasing 6–10 'lucky bean' seeds, < 3cm, black with red-orange cap. **Notes:** Wood reddish-brown, used for canoes, also polishes well for furniture. Leaves and seeds eaten by wildlife. Bark and roots used in traditional medicine. **Other species:** 2 in Zambia: *A. bipindensis* recorded together with *A. peturei* from Mwinilunga gallery forest, possibly the same species.

BEST SEEN
Most national parks
on the plateau and
lower valleys

Baikiaea plurijuga Zambezi Teak

LOCAL NAMES: Mukusyi, Mukusi, Mukushi

A large, semi-deciduous tree, H 27m, S 8–15m, with a tall, straight trunk, erect, spreading lateral branches and a dense canopy. Confined largely to the Kalahari Sand in the west, often dominant. **Bark:** Grey or creamy becoming dark grey-brown, cracked into uniform vertical scales. **Leaves:** Alternate, compound, paripinnate, < 10cm, with 3–6 pairs of opposite, oblong-elliptical leaflets, 5 x 2.5cm, dark glossy green and leathery. Petiole 1–3cm. **Flowers:** Nov–Jun, on axillary racemes, pea-like, 2–3cm, lilac, emerging from velvety-brown, alternate buds. Only 2 or 3 flowers open on each stem and last but a single day.

Fruit: Jun–Nov, flattened, tapering pea-like pods, < 13cm, velvety-brown and leathery, widest at the apex and hooked, splitting explosively, releasing < 3 dark brown seeds. **Notes:** Wood is pinkish to dark red and hard. Used for railway sleepers and parquet flooring, now a valuable export hardwood timber. **Other species:** 4 other species, all in African tropical rainforests. **Vulnerable.**

BEST SEEN
Kalahari Sand woodland and Kafue, Sioma Ngwezi and Liuwa Plain

Bauhinia petersiana **Coffee Bauhinia**

IN ZAMBIA SUBSP. *PETERSIANA*: an untidy, evergreen bush, scrambler or small tree, H 7m, S 2–4m. A common species in drier central, eastern and southern Zambia, frequent in *Baikiaea* forest and Kalahari woodland. **Bark:** Grey-brown, smooth; larger specimens exhibit vertical fissuring. **Leaves:** Distinctly lobed for about half their length and elliptic-ovate, 5 x 6cm, grey-green, with 3–5 pairs of veins from the base. Petiole 2cm. **Flowers:** Dec–Feb, in terminal clusters, 8cm, with 5 feathery-white petals, stamens pinkish. **Fruit:** Jul–Sep, a large, smooth, elongated dehiscent pod, 18cm, brown and woody, splitting explosively.

Notes: Leaves used in traditional medicine as a cold remedy. Seeds used as a coffee substitute by early European explorers. A food plant for several species of moth and butterfly. **Other species:** 6 other species in Zambia: *B. macrantha* and *B. mendoncae* are similar, but confined to Kalahari Sand, with more frilly petals and whitish stamens – all others have pink, purple or red flowers.

BEST SEEN
Baikiaea forest
and all valley
national parks

Brachystegia boehmii Prince of Wales' Feathers

LOCAL NAMES: Ngansa, Musamba, Muombo, Mubombo

A medium-sized semi-evergreen tree, H 18m, S 6–12m, with a short stem, upward-spreading branches and dense, drooping foliage. Twigs hairy. Widespread, often dominant in Miombo on stony soils, and in Kalahari and Mopane woodland. Not in the extreme north or Western Province. An indicator of shallow soils on laterite and rock. **Bark:** Dark grey-brown with shallow but distinct vertical scales. **Leaves:** Alternate, compound, paripinnate, pendulous, with 13–25 opposite pairs of overlapping, oblique, oblong leaflets, 2 x 1cm, olive-green flushing orange-pink, hairy below. Petiole 1cm. **Flowers:** Sep–Nov,

in dense, terminal bunches, < 10cm, greenish-white, sweet-scented, good nectar. **Fruit:** Jun–Nov, a flat, oblong, dehiscent pod, 8–14cm, dark reddish-brown, rounded both ends, beaked, splitting explosively to release 3–6 round, glossy brown seeds. **Notes:** Root fibres used in baskets and fish traps. Inner bark makes a good rope and tannin source. A bee tree, host to some moth species. **Other species:** 17 other species in Zambia, all in Miombo. *B. longifolia* and *B. utilis* are similar, with smaller leaves and fewer leaflets. *B. boehmii* known to hybridise.

BEST SEEN
Plateau and escarpment Miombo woodland including parts of North and South Luangwa

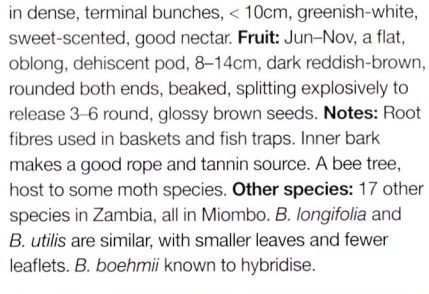

Brachystegia bussei **Munkulungu**

A medium-sized, attractive, deciduous tree, H 20m, S 6–8m, with a short, thick trunk, pale, heavy upward-spreading branches, and an open, round to flattened crown. Occurs across wetter parts in the north. A dominant and gregarious species in Miombo woodland. **Bark:** Purplish-grey and smoothish, but with irregular scales. **Leaves:** Alternate, compound, paripinnate, 5–10cm, with 2–4 opposite pairs of oblique, elliptical-lanceolate leaflets 5 x 3cm, smallest at the base, widely spaced (2cm), bright to grey-green, not glaucous, with secondary veins from base. Flush is bronze or purple. Petiole 1.5–5cm. **Flowers:** Oct–Dec, in tight axillary bunches, < 6cm, small, 5mm, greenish-white, sweet-scented. **Fruit:** Jun–Aug, a flat, oblong, dehiscent 'beaked' pod, 6–9cm, greyish, splitting to release 1–3 flat brown seeds. **Notes:** Bark has an adhesive, dark brown resin. Inner bark used for bark cloth. **Other species:** 17 other species in Zambia, all components of Miombo woodland: similar to *B. spiciformis*, but has leaflets more widely separated, larger and lanceolate, with margins not wavy.

> **BEST SEEN**
> Northern national parks and Miombo woodland

Brachystegia floribunda **Msamba**

LOCAL NAMES: Mubuta, Kasabwa, Musompa, Musobo, Mubombo, Mvukwe

A small to medium-sized, semi-evergreen tree, H 12m, S 6–8m, with a slender trunk, upward-spreading branches, and an open, round crown of 'fluttering' leaves. Twigs are hairy. Occurs across the wetter north, except in the extreme northwest. Locally dominant in plateau Miombo, sometimes in Chipya.
Bark: Pale, uneven, becoming dark grey-brown and fissured, with large rectangular scales. **Leaves:** Alternate, compound, paripinnate with 2–5 opposite pairs of large, half-raised, elliptic leaflets, 8 x 3.5cm, dull blue-green and hairless, flushing scarlet or dark crimson in Sep, widely spaced, with terminal pair largest.

Petiole 4–8cm. **Flowers:** Sep–Nov, in dense terminal bunches on older branches, small, greenish-white and velvety, sweet-scented. **Fruit:** Jun–Sep, a wavy, flat, oblong, woody dehiscent pod, 7–10cm, purple-brown, splitting explosively to release 6–8 round, glossy brown seeds. **Notes:** Root fibres used for baskets and fish traps. Inner bark a good rope and tannin source. A bee tree, also host to several moth species and their larvae. **Other species:** 17 other species in Zambia, all in Miombo: blue-green leaflets distinguish it from *B. bussei* and *B. spiciformis*.

BEST SEEN
Northern national parks and Miombo woodland

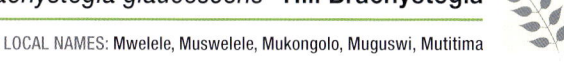

Brachystegia glaucescens Hill Brachystegia

An attractive, medium-sized semi-evergreen tree, H 15m, S 6–20m, with a tall trunk, outward-spreading branches, and an open, flattish crown. Widespread in escarpment Miombo and in granite areas, except in the west. **Bark:** Pale grey and smooth, with sparse, thick, roundish scales peeling to expose yellowish-grey under-bark. Trunk and branches show rounded bulges. **Leaves:** Alternate, compound, paripinnate, 7–9cm, with 9–23 opposite pairs of small, oblique, lanceolate leaflets, 2 x 1cm (with middle ones largest), blue-green, glaucous, with midrib central. Petiole 2–6mm. **Flowers:** Sep–Oct, in short, terminal, branched heads, 4cm, small and creamy-white. **Fruit:** Jun–Sep, a flat, oblong, woody dehiscent pod, 8–13cm, purple-brown, with rounded ends, splitting explosively, releasing 6–8 round, glossy brown seeds in a downward spiral. **Notes:** An attractive tree, but slow-growing and needing sandy soil. Probably fire-intolerant. **Other species:** 17 other species in Zambia, all components of Miombo woodland: *B. microphylla* is similar but with more, smaller leaflets (25–72 pairs), and occurring in higher-rainfall areas.

BEST SEEN
Escarpment and hill zones of most national parks, but not in the west

Brachystegia longifolia Claw-bark Brachystegia

A medium-sized to large semi-evergreen tree, H 30m, S 6–10m, with a tall, straight trunk sometimes swollen at the base, outward-spreading branches, and an open, flattish or rounded crown. Widespread except in the west and the drier parts of the Eastern, Luapula and Northern provinces. Codominant in Miombo and *Cryptosepalum* forest. **Bark:** Dark grey-black with deep vertical, spiralled, claw-mark fissures creating squarish flakes. **Leaves:** Alternate, compound, paripinnate, 7–9cm, with 6–18 opposite pairs of lateral, well-spaced, triangular leaflets, 5 x 1.5cm (middle ones largest), blue-green, leathery, flushing bright red-orange. Petiole 1–1.5cm. **Flowers:** Sep–Dec, in small, terminal, branched heads, 3–4cm, creamy-yellow. **Fruit:** Jun–Sep, a flat, oblong, woody, beaked dehiscent pod, 6–12cm, with rounded ends, reddish-brown, splitting explosively to release 2–6 oval, flat, chestnut-brown seeds. **Notes:** Leaves and bark used in traditional medicine, inner bark for fish traps. A bee tree. **Other species:** 17 other species in Zambia, all in Miombo: *B. boehmii*, *B. utilis*, *B. glaucescens* and *B. stipulata* all similar, but separated by habitat, leaflets smaller, oblique, darker green and leaves with large, leaf-like stipules, respectively.

BEST SEEN
Wetter Miombo
woodland
and northern,
northwestern and
central national parks

Brachystegia microphylla Mountain Acacia

A medium-sized tree, H 35m, but usually smaller, S 6–12m, with a low-branching straight trunk, upward-spreading branches, and an open, flattish, feathery crown. Confined to the wetter north, usually in rocky escarpment Miombo, *Parinari* woodland and mist belts. **Bark:** Grey and smooth, with large flakes falling, leaving depressions and orange-yellow under-bark. **Leaves:** Alternate, compound, paripinnate, 7–9cm, with 25–72 opposite pairs of overlapping, narrow, oblong to triangular leaflets, 10 x 2mm (with middle ones largest), dark green and leathery, flushing pink in Oct. Petiole 1–4mm.

Flowers: Sep–Nov, in loose terminal branched heads, 2–4cm, small, yellow-green and fragrant. **Fruit:** Aug–Oct, a flat, oblong, woody, 'beaked' dehiscent pod, 6–9cm, with rounded ends, dark-brown with a purplish bloom, splitting explosively to release 2–4 oval, flat, brown seeds. **Notes:** Wood is hard and durable. Inner bark makes good string. **Other species:** 17 other species in Zambia, all components of Miombo woodland: *B. glaucescens* and *B. longifolia* are similar but with far fewer leaflets, which are more spaced; *B. stipulata* also similar, but with large, leaf-like stipules at leaf bases.

BEST SEEN
Northern, Luangwa and northwestern national parks and escarpment Miombo

Brachystegia spiciformis **Muputu**

LOCAL NAMES: Manga, Mumuya, Mupanse, Mupuchi, Musewe, Msasa

A large semi-evergreen tree, H 40m, S 6–15m, with a cylindrical trunk, sometimes multi-stemmed, heavy, upward-spreading branches, and a rounded crown. Widespread and abundant, often as a codominant in Miombo, on well-drained soils, also in dry evergreen forest and Kalahari woodland. **Bark:** Grey-brown, smoothish, vertically and horizontally cracked into fine, linking scales. **Leaves:** Alternate, compound, paripinnate and pendulous, 5–20cm, with 2–4 opposite pairs of oblong-elliptical leaflets, 5.5 x 2cm, base asymmetric, with spacing increasing and terminal leaflets

largest, shiny-green, flushing salmon-pink. Petiole 1–5cm. **Flowers:** Aug–Nov, inconspicuous in dense, terminal spikes, 3–8cm, greenish-white producing good nectar, sweet-smelling. **Fruit:** Jun–Nov, a flat, oblong, dehiscent twisting pod, 8–14cm, dark reddish-brown, splitting explosively to release 4–6 round, glossy brown seeds. **Notes:** Bark makes good rope and beehives, contains a tannin used in dyeing; has medicinal properties. A bee tree; host to several butterflies and the edible *ifinkubala* moth larvae, harvested annually. **Other species:** 17 other species in Zambia, all in Miombo: *B. spiciformis* hybridises with *B. glaucescens* and *B. microphylla*.

BEST SEEN

Miombo woodland and almost all national parks, including Sioma Ngwezi and Liuwa Plain

Brachystegia taxifolia   Thicket Brachystegia

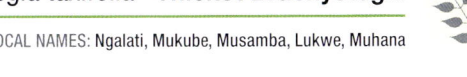

A small to medium-sized evergreen tree, H < 16m but usually smaller, S 6–12m, with a low-branching, layered habit, swollen stem, and dense, flattish crown. Often forms 1.5–2m-high thickets. Confined to the north and east. A possible relict forest species. Often in granite areas, usually in Miombo and Kalahari woodland and dry evergreen forest. **Bark:** Grey-black, smoothish, finely fissured, often encrusted with lichen. **Leaves:** Alternate, compound, paripinnate, 6–12cm, with 20–45 opposite pairs of narrow, oblong to sickle-shaped leaflets, 0.8 x 0.2cm (middle ones largest), spaced at 0.5cm, dark green, flushing orange in Sep. Petiole short. **Flowers:** Aug–Oct, in loose, axillary or terminal branched heads, < 5cm, small, velvet yellow-brown and fragrant. **Fruit:** Jun–Aug, a flat, oblong, woody, 'beaked' dehiscent pod, 4–13cm with rounded ends, pale brown with purplish bloom, splitting explosively to release 2–7 flat brown seeds. **Notes:** Inner bark makes good string. Food plant for several edible caterpillars. Host to Old Man's Beard lichen *Usnea barbata*, which is favoured as nest material by Black-headed Oriole and other Miombo passerines. **Other species:** 17 other species in Zambia, all components of Miombo woodland: similar to *B. microphylla*, but has a distinctive layered growth form.

BEST SEEN
Most Miombo woodland and national parks, but not in the southwest

Burkea africana Red Seringa

LOCAL NAMES: Mukoso, Kapanga, Musese, Mkoso, Museshe

A large deciduous tree, H 10m, S 6–11m, with a tall, straight stem, upward-spreading branches, and an open, rounded crown; dioecious. Young branches with conspicuous rusty hairs. Widespread in most woodland types, commonly in Kalahari woodland. **Bark:** Characteristically grey-brown, uniformly cracked and scaly. Exudes a red or yellow gum when damaged. **Leaves:** Whorled at branch ends, compound, bipinnate with 2–5 pairs of opposite pinnae, with 5–15 alternate, elliptical, papery, leaflets, 4.5 x 2cm, grey-green. Petiole long, 4–10cm. **Flowers:** Aug–Nov, in hanging spikes, < 24cm, small, 5mm, white,

nectar-rich and fragrant. **Fruit:** Apr–Oct, clustered at ends of branchlets, an elliptical, flat, brittle, non-splitting pod, 6–8cm, pale brown and woody, with 1 or 2 flat brown seeds. **Notes:** Wood dark yellow to red-brown, subject to borer attack. Leaves are browsed. Pods and bark are used as a fish poison. The known host for edible caterpillars of *Cirina forda*, *Sphingomorpha chlorea* and 3 others. A good bee tree. **Other species:** A single species across west and southern Africa. *Erythrophleum africanum* and *Albizia antunesiana* similar, but both have denser leaflets and are without rusty-velvety branch tips.

BEST SEEN
All national parks and most woodland areas

Cassia abbreviata Long-pod Cassia

A deciduous shrub or small tree, H 14m, S 4–8m, with an often-crooked, multi-stemmed trunk, and an open, rounded crown; dioecious. Occurs in most woodland types except in the west, often on termite mounds. **Bark:** Reddish becoming dark grey-brown, evenly fissured and cracked. **Leaves:** Compound, paripinnate and drooping, < 30cm, with 7–12 pairs of opposite pinnae, each with 5–15 ovate leaflets, 4 x 2cm, dull green, velvety in new leaflets. Petiole 2.5cm. **Flowers:** Sep–Nov, in open terminal sprays, 15–20cm, large, 4.5cm, yellow and fragrant, appearing before the new leaves. **Fruit:** Dec–Apr, at ends of branchlets, a long, cylindrical pod, < 90cm, velvety-brown, containing numerous separated, flat, brown seeds in sticky pulp. Pods often retained on the tree for several months. **Notes:** Extract of the roots, regarded as poisonous, is sometimes used as a traditional remedy to treat blackwater fever. A food plant for several insect species. Grows easily and makes a good garden plant. **Other species:** 1 other species and 2 subspecies in Zambia: *C. angolensis* has limited distribution. *Senna singueana* is similar but flowers early, has a prominent stalked gland between each pair of leaflets and is usually a shrub with a short, constricted pod.

BEST SEEN
Most woodland areas and all national parks except in western Zambia

Cryptosepalum exfoliatum **Cryptosepalum**

LOCAL NAMES: Mulenda, Musambangalati, Mukwechi, Mukungu, Mukwe

IN ZAMBIA SUBSP. *PSEUDOTAXUS*: a large evergreen tree, H 30m, S 8–15m, with a single trunk, spreading branches, and a dense, flat crown. On sandy soils across the north and northwest; common in the southwest. **Bark:** Grey, becoming dark grey-brown, evenly cracked with small scales. **Leaves:** Alternate, compound, paripinnate, < 10cm, with 4–8 pairs of opposite, small oblong leaflets, 3 x 2cm, dark green and hairy, angled from the rachis. Petiole 2–4cm. **Flowers:** Jun–Sep, in short terminal spikes, 5–8mm, white and fragrant. **Fruit:** Oct–Dec, small oval pods, 3–5cm, brown

with spiked end, containing 2 dark brown seeds. **Notes:** Bark used to make beehives. Inner bark makes good string. Leaves, bark and roots are used in traditional medicine. A good bee tree. Gives its name to the three-storey *Cryptosepalum* forests of Kaoma, Kabompo and Zambezi districts, where it is codominant with *Guibourtia coleosperma*. **Other species:** 5 subspecies and 2 varieties of *C. exfoliatum* in Zambia, plus 1 other species *C. maraviense* (a suffrutex). There are 9 other species occurring from Guinea to Angola.

BEST SEEN
Northern and northwestern national parks; abundant between Kaoma and Kabompo

Daniellia alsteeniana Wild Seringa

LOCAL NAME: Mukulu-busyika

A tall evergreen tree, H 25m, S 8–16m, with a straight trunk, upward-spreading branches and an open, flattened crown; dioecious. Restricted to wetter parts in the north, in Miombo, Chipya and riverine woodland. **Bark:** Characteristically uniformly grey-brown, finely cracked. Yields gum copal when damaged, a type of resin with many uses. **Leaves:** Compound, paripinnate, 11–20cm, with 4–7 pairs of opposite, slightly asymmetrical, lanceolate leaflets, < 7cm, with the middle pair the largest, shiny green, margins wavy. Petiole 2–9cm. **Flowers:** Rarely recorded in Zambia, probably Aug–Nov, on axillary or terminal hanging spikes, < 30cm, with 7–9 lateral branches, < 1.5cm, white and fragrant, stamens long, sepals and inner petals pink. **Fruit:** Oct–Feb, hanging at ends of branchlets, a comma-shaped dehiscent pod, 10–12cm, brown and woody, containing one flat seed, 4–5cm, purplish, attached to the papery endocarp (pit), which acts as a parachute in wind. **Notes:** Wood pinkish-grey, moderate in weight, used for firewood and export timber. Inner bark makes good string. Roots have medicinal properties. **Other species:** 9 other species in equatorial and tropical Africa. **Endangered.**

BEST SEEN
Lusenga Plain
and nearby
Ntumbachushi
Falls and
Kalungwishi River

Erythrophleum africanum   Ordeal Tree

LOCAL NAMES: Kayimbi, Mukoso, Kabulwebulwe, Mubako, Kalunguti, Mungansa

A medium-sized semi-deciduous tree, H 18m, S 5–8m, with a tall, straight trunk, upward-spreading branches and a closed, rounded crown; dioecious. Widespread in most woodland types, not in the Gwembe valley. **Bark:** Reddish, becoming dark grey-brown, with uniform small rectangular scales. Exudes red hardening sap when damaged. **Leaves:** Clustered at branch ends, opposite, compound, bipinnate, with 3 or 4 pairs of opposite pinnae, each with 8–17 alternate, densely arranged, elliptical, papery leaflets, 2.5–5cm, grey-green, velvety below, angled to the rachis. Petiole 1.5–5cm. **Flowers:** Aug–Oct, in

dense, clustered spikes, < 10cm, small, 5mm, white to yellowish with fluffy stamens, sweet-scented and much nectar. **Fruit:** May–Sep, flat, elliptical, dehiscent pods, < 18cm, brown, smooth, splitting back both sides, yielding 1–6 flat glossy brown seeds attached to the pod. **Notes:** Wood reddish-brown, resistant to borers, polishes well. Bark and roots contain a lethal alkaloid. **Other species:** 1 other in Zambia: *E. suaveolens* is similar, with shiny, pointed leaflets with wavy margins, but confined to northern gallery forests. Also similar to *Burkea africana*, which has flaking bark, long petioles and white flowers.

BEST SEEN
Most national parks and most woodland areas

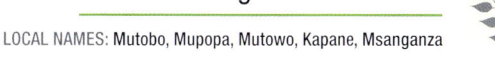

Isoberlinia angolensis Mutobo

IN ZAMBIA VAR. *NIEMBAENSIS*: a medium-sized semi-deciduous tree, H 20m, S 6–10m, with a tall, straight stem, upward-spreading branches, a rounded crown and pods characteristically 'flagging' at the top of the tree. A widespread dominant species across the northern, wetter parts, principally but not exclusively in Miombo woodland. **Bark:** Reddish becoming grey-brown, rough and extensively cracked and scaly, patchy where scales have dropped. Exudes a reddish sap. **Leaves:** Alternate, compound, paripinnate, with 3 or 4 opposite pairs of large, ovate to oblong leaflets, 10 x 5cm, dull grey-green, sometimes hairy below, with terminal pair largest. Petiole 3–5cm.

Flowers: Sep–Dec, sometimes Mar–May, showy sprays, with large, fluffy stamens, 2cm, white to yellowish, producing much nectar. **Fruit:** Aug–Oct, a long, flat, oblong, dehiscent pod, 10–18cm, golden-velvety, splitting explosively to release 4–6 large, flat, round, pale seeds. **Notes:** Inner bark makes good string and an infusion used for toothache. A bee tree. Also host to several edible caterpillars. **Other species:** 1 other species in Zambia: *I. tomentosa* is similar and, like the 2 other varieties of *I. angolensis*, differentiated by the flowering parts.

BEST SEEN
Most national parks, but not in the west

Julbernardia globiflora **Mpasa**

LOCAL NAMES: Mpasa, Katondomumba, Mwanza, Kabunga, Kamponi, Mumba

A medium-sized semi-evergreen tree, H 18m, S 6–8m, with a cylindrical trunk, crooked branches, a closed crown, and pods characteristically 'flagging' at the top of the tree as in *Isoberlinia*. Common and widespread at medium and lower altitudes in escarpment Miombo woodland, on rocky slopes and poor soils, except in the northwest and west. Often a codominant with *Brachystegia* species. **Bark:** Pale grey and smooth, becoming dark brown, rough, and extensively cracked and scaly (similar to *Isoberlinia*). Exudes a reddish sap when damaged. **Leaves:** Alternate, compound,

paripinnate, with 4–7 opposite lateral pairs of oblong-lanceolate leaflets, 5 x 2cm, dull green, diagnostic fine hairs around margins. Petiole 3cm. **Flowers:** Feb–May, also Oct–Nov, in branched heads, 6–30cm, at the top of the tree (similar to *Isoberlinia*), but inconspicuous, 5mm, white, fragrant and producing much nectar. **Fruit:** Jul–Nov, flat and characteristically flat-ended, 'beaked', dehiscent pods, 10–18cm, velvety-brown, splitting explosively to release 2–6 large, flat, round, smooth, brown seeds. **Notes:** Bark contains a tannin used in dyes. A good bee tree, also host to several moth larvae. Dwarf forms sometimes found. **Other species:** 1 other species in Zambia: *J. paniculata* and *Brachystegia spiciformis* are similar, but have fewer than 4 pairs of elliptical, shiny-green leaflets.

> **BEST SEEN**
> All national parks
> in the north, east
> and south

Julbernardia paniculata **Mutondo**

LOCAL NAMES: Mutondo, Muchesa, Mwanda, Mtondo

A medium-sized to large semi-evergreen tree, H 23m, S 6–10m, with a cylindrical trunk, sometimes multi-stemmed, an upward-branching habit and a rounded crown. Widespread and very common and gregarious, except in drier areas. Occurs principally in Miombo woodland where it is often the dominant species, also in dry evergreen forest and Kalahari woodland. **Bark:** Grey-brown, smoothish, flaking in squarish scales and leaving blotchy, pale under-bark. **Leaves:** Alternate, compound, paripinnate, with 2–4 opposite pairs of oblong leaflets, 10 x 3cm, shiny green with diagnostic fine hairs around margins.

Petiole 3–5cm. **Flowers:** Mar–Jul, after *J. globiflora*, in large, oblique, branched heads, 25cm, at the top of branches, inconspicuous, 1.5cm, creamy-white. Producing good nectar. **Fruit:** Aug–Nov, a flat, oblong, dehiscent pod, 5–11cm, dark brown, with a characteristic 'beak', splitting explosively to release up to 4 large, flat, round, smooth, brown seeds.

Notes: Bark makes a good rope, used for binding thatch bundles. An infusion is used to relieve cold symptoms; also contains a tannin used in dyeing. A good bee tree, yielding prized Mutondo honey. A host to these popular edible moth larvae: *ifinkubala*, Banded Emporer *Cinabra hyperbius* and Mopane Worm *Gonimbrasia belina*. **Other species:** 1 other species in Zambia: *J. globiflora*. *Brachystegia spiciformis* is similar, but has smaller leaflets without fringing hairs.

> **BEST SEEN**
> Miombo woodland, including most national parks, but not in the west

Peltophorum africanum   African Wattle

LOCAL NAMES: Mwikalankanga, Mulungwa, Mwezenyele, Mteta, Muzenzenze

A medium-sized to large semi-deciduous tree, H 30m, S 6–15m, sometimes multi-stemmed or with a crooked trunk, having numerous branches and a feathery crown. Widespread in most woodland types, but particularly abundant in Munga woodland and around *Baikiaea* forest. **Bark:** Light brown, horizontally striated, becoming rough with vertical scales. **Leaves:** Opposite, compound, bipinnate, 4–9 pairs of opposite pinnae, each with 8–20 pairs of small oblong leaflets, 7 x 2mm, dull green, paler below. Petiole 2–5cm, with dense rusty hairs. **Flowers:** Sep–Jan, showy in dense, axillary sprays,

< 15cm, bright yellow with a citrus smell, producing very good nectar. **Fruit:** Apr–Sep, in dense clusters, a flat elliptical pod, 5–10cm, brown, with narrow winged margins, containing 1 or 2 round, brown seeds. **Notes:** A good bee tree, also a 'rain tree'. Host to several butterflies and moth larvae. Grows easily and makes a good shade tree in a garden. **Other species:** None in Zambia. Only 1 species indigenous to Africa. *P. africanum* similar to *Acacia amythethophylla* (= *Vachellia amythethophylla*), but the latter sparsely spiny and flowers are yellow-orange balls.

BEST SEEN
Munga woodland
in Luangwa and all
national parks in
the south and west

Piliostigma thonningii **Monkeybread**

A medium-sized deciduous tree, H 15m, S 6–12m, sometimes multi-stemmed or with a crooked trunk, heavy branches drooping at the ends and an open crown. Occurs widely in most woodland types and wooded grassland, absent from forest and montane habitats. Abundant in Munga and Chipya woodland. **Bark:** Grey-brown, rough, vertically and spirally striated. **Leaves:** Simple, alternate, large, < 12cm, distinctly 2-lobed, with 4–6 veins radiating from base. Petiole thick, 2–4cm. **Flowers:** Nov–Mar, in hanging axillary or terminal sprays, small, 1.5cm, white and fragrant, with a velvety calyx. **Fruit:** May–Sep, a large, flat, oblong, indehiscent pod, < 22cm, brown, falling usually without splitting, with numerous round, glossy brown seeds in an edible floury matrix (hence 'monkeybread'). **Notes:** Leaves and fruit favoured by wildlife. Bark yields a dye and good rope. Ash used as a soap substitute. Host to several butterfly and moth larvae. Grows easily and makes a good shade tree. **Other species:** None in Zambia; 2 others in tropical Africa, Australia and Asia. Leaf shape similar to some *Bauhinia* species but their leaves are generally smaller.

BEST SEEN
All national parks except Nyika and common in Munga woodland

Senna singueana Winter Cassia

LOCAL NAMES: **Kafungunashya, Mululu, Muninyampuku, Mtantanyelele, Mululwe**

A deciduous shrub or small tree, H 11m, S 3–8m, usually multi-stemmed, often with a crooked trunk, untidy branches and an open crown. Occurs widely in all woodland types and wooded grassland but absent from wetter forest and montane habitats. Particularly abundant in Munga and Chipya woodland, often in large stands on alluvium. **Bark:** Grey-brown, fissured and cracked. **Leaves:** Alternate, compound, paripinnate, < 20cm, with 4–10 pairs of leaflets, opposite, 4 x 1.5cm, fresh-green and velvety, with conspicuous glands between each pair (unlike *Cassia abbreviata*). Petiole 1.5–5cm.

Flowers: Mar–Nov, before *Cassia abbreviata*, in large sprays, 15–20cm, bright yellow and fragrant. **Fruit:** Sep–Jun, in clusters, thin, cylindrical, constricted pods, < 20 x 0.5cm, yellow becoming black. Seeds numerous round, glossy brown in sticky matrix. **Notes:** A fire-tolerant species, not utilised by wildlife. Has potential as a garden specimen. **Other species:** 5 other species in Zambia: 3 are cultivated shrubs, 1 a wasteland species. *S. petersiana* is similar, but has tapering, pointed leaflets and flattened, hairy pods; it is usually a dambo species.There is also a possible hybrid of *S. singueana* x *S. petersiana*.

BEST SEEN
Most national parks except Nyika and common in Munga woodland

Tamarindus indica Tamarind

LOCAL NAMES: Mushishi, Mwemba, Musika

A medium-sized to large evergreen tree, H 25m, S 5–12m, usually branching early, with drooping branches and a dense, feathery crown. Occurs at low altitudes in the Tanganyika-Mweru, Luangwa and lower Zambezi rifts, in escarpment streamlines, and riparian and alluvial woodland, often on termitaria. **Bark:** Light to dark grey, rough, vertically striated with small reptile-like scales. **Leaves:** Alternate, compound, paripinnate, < 20cm, with 10–18 opposite pairs of leaflets, 1.5 x 0.8cm, grey-green and hairless, with prominent veins. Petiole short, 1.5cm. **Flowers:** Oct–May, striking, on long spikes at branch ends, orchid-like, pale yellow and red, usually with 1 flower and several red buds. **Fruit:** Jul–Nov, in clusters, a sausage-shaped indehiscent pod, 10–18cm, leathery but brittle, velvety, constricted between seeds and often curled. Seeds glossy brown in sticky, fibrous, acidic edible pulp. **Notes:** Wood polishes well. Leaves favoured by many wildlife species that also use the shade. Fruit pulp rich in vitamin C, also used to make porridge. A slow-growing garden tree. **Other species:** A single species across the Old World tropics. Possibly introduced from Asia by early Indian Ocean traders.

> **BEST SEEN**
> Nsumbu, North and South Luangwa and Lower Zambezi national parks

Baphia massaiensis **Sand Camwood**

IN ZAMBIA SUBSP. *OBOVATA*: a small to medium-sized evergreen tree, H 10m, S 3–5m, with a fluted, twisted trunk, upward-spreading branches, and a dense, rounded crown; dioecious. Occasional in low- to medium-altitude woodland and valleys, usually on sandy soils, common in *Baikiaea* woodland. **Bark:** Creamy to dark brown with scales, branchlets hairy. **Leaves:** Alternate, compound, unifoliate, with a single leaflet emerging from a swelling on the stem at the base of the petiole, ovate, 7 x 3cm, dark green and leathery, hairless above and greyish hairs below. Petiole 3.5cm. **Flowers:** Oct–Feb, in short sprays, 5–10cm, pea-like with pink sepals, and white petals with yellow patch at the base, sweet-smelling. **Fruit:** Jul–Aug, a smooth, flat pod, < 12cm, with pointed tip, red-brown. **Notes:** Wood is yellowish, prone to borers. Pounded roots give a soap, and roots and leaves are used for skin ailments. A nitrogen-fixing pioneer species in abandoned cassava fields. **Other species:** 4 in Zambia: *B. bequaertii*, *B. multiflora* and *B. speciosa* are northern species. *B. whitei* occurs in the northwest; 45 other species across tropical Africa and Madagascar.

BEST SEEN
Most valley national parks on sandy and alluvial soils

Bobgunnia madagascariensis **Snake Bean**

LOCAL NAMES: Ndale, Musyaka-seyela, Kapwipu, Mchelekete, Mulundu

A small semi-deciduous tree, H 15m, S 3–5m, with a straightish trunk, twisted branches, and an open, rounded crown. Occasional in most woodland types at low to medium altitudes. **Bark:** Grey-black with a lattice of vertical fissures. **Leaves:** Alternate, compound, imparipinnate, with 5–11 alternate to subopposite oblong-elliptic leaflets, 5 x 2cm, leathery, dark green above, yellowish and hairy below. Petiole < 3cm. **Flowers:** Sep–Nov, often longer, , in branched sprays, with a single, large white petal, 1.5–2cm and numerous yellow-orange stamens, sweet-scented. **Fruit:** May–Sep, a long, cylindrical, curved, indehiscent wooden pod, < 30cm, glossy black, with 10–15 seeds between gummy partitions.

Notes: Wood reddish-brown, used in carving. Pods and seeds used as a fish poison and to kill bilharzia snails, but also eaten by wildlife. Roots, bark, leaves and seeds are used in traditional medicine to relieve headaches and heart palpitations. A host species for some butterflies. **Other species:** This species occurs as a single taxon across tropical and southern Africa, but not in Madagascar, despite the scientific name.

Bolusanthus speciosus Tree Wisteria

LOCAL NAME: Masunga

A graceful, small to medium-sized semi-deciduous tree, H 8m, S 2–4m, often multi-stemmed, with drooping foliage. Occasional in most southern woodlands at low to medium altitudes, usually on sandier soils. **Bark:** Light to dark brown with deep vertical fissures. **Leaves:** Alternate, compound, imparipinnate, with 3–7 pairs of opposite lanceolate leaflets, < 7 x 1cm, shiny, grey-green, but dull green below, with tiny silvery hairs and an asymmetrical base. Terminal leaflet, midrib and veins distinctive and yellowish. Petiole 5–10cm. **Flowers:** Aug–Nov, sometimes longer, in terminal sprays, < 30cm,

attractive, drooping pea-shaped, blue-mauve. **Fruit:** Feb–May, in clusters, a long, thin, papery and partly dehiscent pod, < 10cm, brown. Containing 3–8 smooth seeds, bright yellow or brown. **Notes:** Wood reddish-brown, valued for carving and furniture. Roots and bark used in traditional medicine for abdominal complaints. A favoured garden tree. **Other species:** This species occurs as a single taxon across southern and central Africa. **Protected in South Africa.**

BEST SEEN

Kafue and Zambezi valley national parks; occasionally in plateau woodland

Cordyla africana **Wild Mango**

A large, deciduous and sometimes semi-deciduous tree, H 25m, S < 20m, with a short trunk, often branching at a low height, and a wide-spreading crown; mono- or dioecious. Occurs in riverine woodland at low altitudes in eastern, central and southern Zambia. **Bark:** Grey to dark brown with distinct raised vertical ridges. Exudes a resin when damaged. **Leaves:** Alternate, compound, imparipinnate, with 11–28 usually alternate, oblong leaflets, 4 x 2cm, shiny green above and paler below. Petiole 1.5–2.5cm. **Flowers:** Jul–Oct, in short, dense, axillary upward-facing sprays, < 30cm, hemispherical heads, 2.5cm, with orange-yellow stamens, without petals. **Fruit:** Nov–May, a fleshy, ovoid drupe, 4–8cm, green-yellow ripening to bright yellow on the ground. Containing 1 or 2 large seeds that germinate inside. **Notes:** Wood used for canoes and drums. Fruit is high in vitamin C and can be eaten fresh or cooked. Relished by primates, elephants and other herbivores. **Other species:** 4 in coastal and low-altitude riverine habitats in tropical Africa and Madagascar.

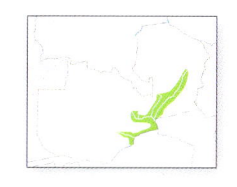

BEST SEEN

Riverine areas in most national parks in the north, east and south

Craibia brevicaudata Mountain Craibia

LOCAL NAMES: Mupande, Mpange

IN ZAMBIA SUBSP. *BAPTISTARUM*: a medium-sized to large evergreen tree, H 18m, S < 12m, with trunk sometimes buttressed or fluted, branching upwards, and a dense, rounded crown with drooping edges. Confined to wetter north and northeast, typically in riverine and montane forest, and relict evergreen thicket. **Bark:** Pale grey and smooth, becoming scaly, with square flakes. **Leaves:** Alternate, compound, imparipinnate, with 5–7 alternate, elliptic to oblong-lanceolate leaflets, 9 x 2.5cm, shiny dark green and leathery, with apex tapering and margin wavy. Petiole grooved. **Flowers:** Oct–Jan, at branch ends, in showy, short dense sprays, < 15cm, flowers sweet-pea-like, white with a pink tinge. **Fruit:** May–Jun, a flat, asymmetrically tapering dehiscent pod, 8–10cm, green to creamy-grey and becoming dark brown, opening explosively to release 1 or 2 large, glossy reddish seeds, which travel < 15m. **Notes:** Wood used for furniture. No other known uses. Difficult to grow, but makes an attractive specimen tree. **Other species:** 2 in Zambia: *C. affinis* is similar, but with more lanceolate leaflets; *C. grandiflora* has longer and wider leaflets and is confined to northern forests.

BEST SEEN
Nyika and
Lusenga Plain

Dalbergia melanoxylon **Blackwood**

A shrub or small, spiny, semi-deciduous tree, H 5–15m, S < 8m, with an often-crooked or multi-stemmed trunk, with upward-spreading then drooping branches, and a dense crown. Confined to the drier centre, south and east. Typically in thickets in Mopane and Munga woodland, but also in rocky areas and on termite mounds. **Bark:** Pale grey and smooth becoming dark grey and scaly, shedding square flakes. Spines straight. Exudes red gum when damaged. **Leaves:** Compound, imparipinnate, clustered along branchlets, with 7–13, opposite or alternate, heart-shaped or oval leaflets, 1.5 x 1cm, dark green and leathery, with base tapering. Petiole short.

Flowers: Oct–Dec, with first rains, at branch ends in showy, short, branched dense sprays, < 10cm, small, pea-like, white, sweet-scented. **Fruit:** Jan–Mar, a small, flattened, papery, oblong indehiscent pod, < 7cm, swollen around the 1 or 2 large, brown seeds. **Notes:** Heartwood purplish becoming black, valued for small carvings. Roots used to reduce toothache. **Other species:** 8 similar species in Zambia, 6 of which are climbers: *D. nitidula* has fewer leaflets, and often has clustered black galls on smaller branches; *D. boehmii* has no spines.

BEST SEEN
Inconspicuous, but in most parks with Mopane or *Combretum–Terminalia* woodland

Dalbergiella nyasae Mane Pod

LOCAL NAMES: Kakwete, Mukula-mnsinga, Kafwango, Msansale, Kafunda, Mwamba

An untidy, medium-sized deciduous tree, H 5–12m, S < 8m, with a sometimes-flattened trunk, upward-spreading then drooping branches, and an open crown. Widespread, but absent from the northwest and southwest, most common in Miombo and Kalahari woodland and escarpments, also in Mopane and Munga woodland. **Bark:** Grey-brown to dark brown, vertically fissured. Branchlets with golden hairs. Exudes a crimson gum when damaged. **Leaves:** Spirally arranged, crowded at branch ends or on stem, compound, imparipinnate, 6–15 opposite or subopposite, asymmetric, oval or oblong leaflets, 4 x 2cm,

grey-green, rounded at both base and apex, with middle leaflets largest. Petiole short. **Flowers:** Aug–Oct, before new leaves, showy, spectacular drooping sprays, 25cm, of small pea-like flowers, whitish-pink with a mauve spot on the main petal, sweet-scented. **Fruit:** Sep–Nov, an oblong, flattened, indehiscent pod, 6–8cm, velvety-yellowish and leathery, distinctively fringed with dense, reddish-brown hairs. Swollen around 1 or 2 large, brown seeds. **Notes:** Bark is used as a fish poison. Would make an interesting ornamental garden tree. Leaves of *Dalbergia* species are similar but their leaflets are neither oblong nor rounded at both ends. **Other species:** None in Zambia; 2 in Africa.

BEST SEEN
Kafue, also present in eastern and southern national parks

Erythrina abyssinica Lucky Bean Tree

A medium-sized, spiny, deciduous tree, H 5–15m, S < 10m, with a short trunk, stout branches, and a rounded, open crown. Widespread in wooded grassland, rocky areas and Chipya woodland. Absent in evergreen forest and Kalahari Sand. **Bark:** Grey-brown to dark brown, corky and vertically fissured, often with spiny-tipped knobs on the trunk and hooked prickles on the smaller branches. Exudes a brown gum when damaged. **Leaves:** Compound, trifoliate, with ovate leaflets, 10 x 10cm, terminal leaflet largest, dull grey-green, paler and usually hairy below, sometimes with scattered prickles on the midrib. Petiole 10–15cm.

Flowers: Jul–Oct, emerging simultaneously when the tree is leafless, in showy scarlet terminal spikes. **Fruit:** Nov–Mar, a curled, necklace-like pod, < 10cm, very constrained between the seeds, dark brown or blackish, furry, splitting to release 2–6 bright scarlet and black seeds ('lucky beans'). **Notes:** Wood light-coloured, used to make toys and drums. Seeds used in necklaces and trinkets. Seed pulp contains toxic alkaloids, lethal only if injected. Grows well from truncheons; a good garden specimen tree. **Other species:** 6 in Zambia: *E. latissima* is similar, but has larger, overlapping leaflets; *E. livingstoniana* leaves are lobed, not trifoliate; 2 are riverine (*mushitu*) trees and others are suffrutices.

BEST SEEN
All national parks except in the west, most visible in Kafue

Pericopsis angolensis Mubanga

A medium-sized to large deciduous tree, H 20m, S < 10m, with a variable trunk, erect but crooked branches, and a rounded, open crown. Widespread at low and medium altitudes, but not in Mopane woodland. **Bark:** Reddish-brown becoming pale grey, smooth becoming scaly, with irregular peeling flakes. **Leaves:** Alternate, compound, imparipinnate, with 7–10 subopposite or alternate ovate-elliptic leaflets, 5 x 2.5cm, dark green and leathery, apex rounded. Petiole 2–4cm. **Flowers:** Sep–Nov, attractive pea-like flowers in terminal branched sprays, < 15cm, small, pale pink-purple and veined.

Fruit: Jul–Sep, in clusters, a flat, oblong, tapering indehiscent pod, often thinly winged, very variable, 7–24cm, light brown, releasing 1 or 2 flat, orange or reddish seeds. **Notes:** A fire-resistant species producing a valuable but hard timber. Leaves, flowers and fruit are browsed by wildlife. Leaves and bark are used in traditional medicine for headache relief. **Other species:** 3 other species, mostly in tropical Africa. Similar to *Xeroderris stuhlmannii*, which has larger and fewer leaflets, broader wings on the pod, and is confined to the lower, drier, south of Zambia.

BEST SEEN
All valley
national parks

Philenoptera violacea Rain Tree

LOCAL NAMES: Mufundwe-lamba, Chimpakasa, Mupanda, Muhulu, Mukololo

A medium-sized to large semi-deciduous tree, H 20m, S < 10m, with a straight trunk, erect branches drooping at ends, and a patchy, rounded crown. Common and widespread in most woodland types at low and medium altitudes, but not in the northwest. **Bark:** Pale grey, smooth becoming cracked and scaly. Exudes a crimson sap when damaged. **Leaves:** Alternate, compound, imparipinnate, with 1 or 2 pairs of opposite, oblong-ovate leaflets, 10 x 5cm, glossy green above and grey-green below, leathery, terminal leaflet much larger, apex with a single fine hair, young leaves hairy. Petiole 2–4cm. **Flowers:** Aug–Nov, in fragrant terminal sprays, < 30cm, showy, small pea-like flowers, mauve. **Fruit:** May–Oct, in untidy clusters, a flat, indehiscent pod, 7–15cm, often thinly winged, with sharp ends, creamy-grey, with 1–5 kidney-shaped seeds. **Notes:** Leaves, flowers and fruit browsed by wildlife. Roots used in traditional medicine for leprosy sores; also contain rotenone, a broad-spectrum insecticide. Called a 'rain tree' after the copious moisture drops falling from the spittle bug *Ptyelus grossus*. Supports a long and copious honey flow. **Other species:** 5 in Zambia, leaves either trifoliate or imparipinnate, but with more than 2 pairs of leaflets.

BEST SEEN
Most valley
national parks

Pterocarpus angolensis Mukwa

LOCAL NAMES: Mulombwa, Mukulakula, Mukwa, Mlombe

A medium-sized to large deciduous tree, H 25m, S < 15m, with a straight trunk, upward-branching habit and open, rounded crown. Widespread in all woodlands. **Bark:** Variable grey-brown to black, vertically cracked with scaly ridges. Exudes a crimson sap when damaged. **Leaves:** Alternate, compound, imparipinnate, with 5–9 pairs of opposite or subopposite, ovate to elliptic-lanceolate leaflets, 5 x 3cm, dark green above, paler below, with apex tapering, margins wavy, and a bristle tip. Petiole 5–10cm. Leafless for up to 4 months. **Flowers:** Aug–Oct, in branched, terminal sprays, < 20cm, small, showy, pea-like, orange-yellow,

fragrant. **Fruit:** Mar–Jun, staying on the tree, a flat, indehiscent, circular pod, < 15cm, resembling a light brown fried egg, with bristly central seed case holding 1 or 2 glossy brown seeds, opened by fire or termites. **Notes:** Wood reddish-brown with white sapwood; has been heavily exploited for furniture and as an export timber, so stocks heavily depleted. Roots, bark and leaves have medicinal uses. Resin used as fish poison. **Other species:** 4 in Zambia, 1 subspecies: *P. rotundifolius* has no hairs over central seed base; *P. tinctorius* is similar, but has reddish bark, overlapping leaflets. **Least Concern.**

BEST SEEN
All national parks

Xeroderris stuhlmannii Wing Pod

A medium-sized deciduous tree, H 23m, S < 14m, with often-crooked trunk and branches, and a spreading, dense crown; dioecious. Confined to the drier east and south at low to medium altitudes, mainly in Munga woodland, but occasionally in other woodland types. **Bark:** Variable grey-brown, with roundish scales. Exudes a crimson sap when damaged. **Leaves:** Spiralled at the tips of branches, compound, imparipinnate, with 4–15 pairs of opposite or subopposite, asymmetric, oblong-ovate leaflets, 9 x 4.5cm, blue-green, creased along the midrib, apex rounded, hairy when young. Petiole < 10cm.

Flowers: Sep–Nov, in showy, branched terminal sprays, < 20cm, pea-like, white or greenish, with rust-coloured buds. **Fruit:** May–Aug, in clusters, a flat, indehiscent pod, 10–18cm, with broad wings on margins, brown, swollen and veined over 1–4 brown seeds. **Notes:** Wood dark yellow and light, but splits. Pods and leaves browsed by elephant and antelope. Bark and gum produce a red dye, also used in tanning. **Other species:** A single-species genus in tropical Africa: *Pericopsis angolensis* (Mubanga) is similar, but has smaller, alternate leaflets, so terminal leaflet less distinct.

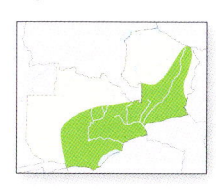

BEST SEEN
Most southern valley
national parks

Entandrophragma caudatum   **Wooden Banana**

LOCAL NAMES: Mofu, Mulolo, Mupumena, Mpanje, Nabalali, Mungovu

A tall deciduous tree, H 30m, S 8–15m, with a straight trunk, sometimes buttressed, < 2m wide, untidily branching, with a rounded crown. Confined to the drier, sandier southern half, often in riverside and Munga woodland, but also in other habitats. **Bark:** Greyish, rough, with plate-like scales, 12cm, peeling, revealing pale under-bark. **Leaves:** Clustered at branch ends, compound, paripinnate, with 5–8 pairs of ovate-lanceolate drooping leaflets, 11cm, dark green above, paler below, and the apex with a thin point. Petiole 4cm. Leafless May–Aug. **Flowers:** Aug–Oct, in loose terminal sprays, 20cm, inconspicuous,

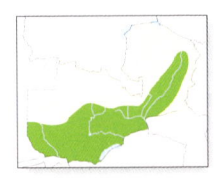

white to yellowish-green. **Fruit:** Jul–Sep, a long woody capsule, < 15cm, light brown, splitting into 5 segments and curling back to release 40 winged seeds. **Notes:** Litunga's canoe in Western Province is made from this tree. Timber has high commercial demand, but resources are diminishing. **Other species:** 2 in Zambia: *E. delevoyi* and *E. excelsum* are both tall, high-rainfall species in northern habitats. *E. delevoyi* is a **Vulnerable** species and similar to *E. caudatum*, but has more tapering leaflets and the capsule splits from its tip.

BEST SEEN
Lower Zambezi,
Kafue and
Sioma Ngwezi

Khaya nyasica Red Mahogany

A large evergreen shade tree, H 40m, S 8–25m, with a sometimes-swollen or buttressed straight trunk, heavy, upward-spreading branches, and a dense rounded crown. Widespread at medium and low altitudes in evergreen forest and riparian woodland, except in western Kalahari Sand areas. **Bark:** Grey-brown or darker, fairly smooth, but dimpled, sometimes horizontally ringed and flaking. **Leaves:** Spirally arranged, compound, paripinnate, with 2–7 pairs of oblong-elliptical leaflets, < 17cm, glossy dark green above, paler below and leathery, apex a thin point. Petiole < 12cm. New leaves reddish. **Flowers:** Sep–Nov, in loose axillary sprays, 20cm, small, 10mm, white and sweet-scented. **Fruit:** Jun–Oct, a round woody capsule, 3–5cm, grey, splitting into 4 or 5 valves, curling back to release 30–60 winged seeds. **Notes:** Widely planted along urban streets. The reddish wood is in demand for the timber trade, but supply is limited. **Other species:** 6 in tropical Africa and Madagascar: *K. nyasica* similar to *Trichilia emetica*, which is smaller and with imparipinnate leaflets. **Near Threatened.**

> **BEST SEEN**
> Riverine areas of
> most national parks

Acacia galpinii Monkey Thorn

LOCAL NAMES: Kwikala-nkanga, Mkunku, Nombe

(= *SENEGALIA GALPINII*) A large deciduous tree, H 25m, S 20m, with a straight trunk, upward-spreading branches and a diffuse crown. From the Copperbelt, south- and westward, in wooded grassland and along riverbanks. **Bark:** Pale and flaky, becoming dark brown, corky, with vertical furrows. Thorns in opposite pairs, short, broad and hooked, < 10cm. **Leaves:** Alternate, compound, bipinnate, < 11cm, with 9–14 pairs of opposite pinnae, the middle pinnae largest, each with 13–40 opposite pairs of oblong, symmetric, overlapping leaflets, 8 x 2mm, dark green, hairless. Petiole 1.5–4cm. **Flowers:** Sep–Oct, in

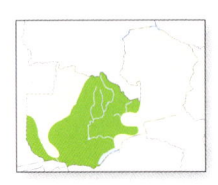

long, 10cm, cream to yellow spikes, with unusual reddish calyxes before the flowers open. Appearing with the new leaves. **Fruit:** Feb–Mar, a large, straight, dehiscent pod, 28cm, purple-brown, thickened at the seed points, releasing 6–11 red-purple seeds. **Notes:** Flowers attract bees; seed pods are browsed by herbivores. A large tree affording good shade. **Other species:** 27 in Zambia and 8 subspecies: now separated into 14 *Vachellia* species (pom-pom flowers) and 13 *Senegalia* species (flowers borne in spikes). Similar to *Acacia polyacantha* but has overlapping, not separated, leaflets.

BEST SEEN
Wooded grasslands and central, southern and western national parks

Acacia nigrescens Knob Thorn

LOCAL NAMES: **Nyamponondwe, Mukwena, Kankande, Mwaba**

(= *SENEGALIA NIGRESCENS*) A medium-sized to large deciduous tree, H 20m, S 6–12m, with a rounded or spreading crown, and its knob-like thorns on the trunk and branches. Widespread at low and medium altitudes in open savanna or Munga woodland. Not in the north. **Bark:** Dark brown to black, fissured and ridged with distinctive knobs tipped by small, paired, hooked thorns. **Leaves:** Alternate, compound, bipinnate, with 1–4 pairs of pinnae, each with 1 or 2 pairs of large, oval to circular leaflets, 2 x 1.5cm, grey-green, leathery. Often leafless for several months. **Flowers:** Aug–Nov, in clustered spikes, 10cm, white and fragrant. Before the new leaves. **Fruit:** Jul–Sep, a long, thin, straight, dehiscent pod, < 16cm, red-brown, tapering to the stem. Pods explode releasing 2–6 green-brown seeds with horseshoe markings. **Notes:** Drought-resistant. Bark makes good rope. Protein-rich leaves and fruit eaten by domestic animals and wildlife. Flowers attract bees. A large garden specimen tree with a non-aggressive root system; it drops thorny stems. **Other species:** 27 in Zambia and 8 subspecies: now separated into 14 *Vachellia* species (pom-pom flowers) and 13 *Senegalia* species (flowers borne in spikes).

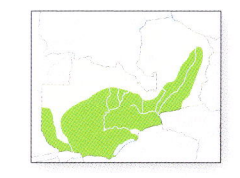

BEST SEEN
Most national parks

Acacia polyacantha **White Thorn**

LOCAL NAMES: **Munganunshi, Chibombo, Mukotokoto, Chombwe, Ngowe, Mumbu**

(= *SENEGALIA POLYACANTHA*) IN ZAMBIA SUBSP. *POLYACANTHA*: a medium-sized to large deciduous tree, H 20m, S 15m, with a straight trunk, upward-spreading branches, and an open, leafy, layered crown. Widespread, relatively short-lived, often a pioneer species invading degraded land. Typically at low and medium altitudes in wooded grassland, dambos and valleys. **Bark:** Yellowish-brown, flaking in corky blocks or loose strips, with woody bosses. Hooked thorns most evident on young branches. Exudes a gum when damaged. **Leaves:** Alternate, compound, bipinnate, < 24cm, with 15–40 pairs of opposite pinnae, middle

pinnae largest, with 20–60 pairs of small, triangular leaflets, 3 x 0.5mm, light green. Petiole short 0.5–4cm. **Flowers:** Sep–Dec, in long spikes, < 12cm, white, fragrant; with the new leaves. **Fruit:** Jun–Oct, in bunches at branch ends, a straight, thin, woody dehiscent pod, 7–18cm, dark brown, tapering at both ends, slightly curved, splitting to release 6–8 flat, brown seeds. **Notes:** Flowers attract bees. Gum used in dyeing and as pottery pigment. Pods and bark high in protein, browsed by herbivores. A nitrogen-fixing plant. **Other species:** 27 in Zambia and 8 subspecies: now separated into 14 *Vachellia* species (pom-pom flowers) and 13 *Senegalia* species (flowers borne in spikes).

BEST SEEN
Disturbed plateau woodland and most national parks

LOCAL NAMES: **Lupangala, Mpamba, Umunga**

(= *VACHELLIA KARROO*) A small to medium-sized evergreen tree, H 15m, S 6–10m, with upward-spreading branches, and a dense, rounded crown. Confined to central Zambia, in Munga and riverine woodland, usually on good loamy soils, occasionally in Miombo woodland. **Bark:** Young branches distinctly orange-red and smooth, becoming dark brown, rough and fissured. Thorns at nodes, paired, opposite, straight, < 5cm, whitish with dark tips. **Leaves:** Alternate, compound, bipinnate, with 2–5 pairs of pinnae, each with 8–20 pairs of small leaflets, 6 x 2.5mm, dark green. Petiole short. **Flowers:** Nov–Feb, clustered at branch ends, on long axillary or terminal stems, small balls, < 5cm, bright golden yellow and fragrant. **Fruit:** Jan onwards, a slender, sickle-shaped, thinly woody, dehiscent pod, < 16cm, red-brown with a purplish bloom, constricted between seeds, splitting on the tree to release 5–8 flat, brown seeds. **Notes:** A quick-yielding wood producer, with leaves providing good fodder for browsers. Inner bark makes good rope. Gum is red and edible. A good bee tree and garden tree, growing easily from seed, but it does drop thorns. **Other species:** 27 in Zambia and 8 subspecies: now separated into 14 *Vachellia* species (pom-pom flowers) and 13 *Senegalia* species (flowers borne in spikes).

> **BEST SEEN**
> Kafue and central plateau woodland on loam soils

Acacia nilotica Scented-pod Thorn

LOCAL NAMES: **Kafifi, Uzimwi, Nombe**

(= *VACHELLIA NILOTICA*) IN ZAMBIA SUBSP. *KRAUSSIANA*: a small to medium-sized semi-deciduous tree, H 10m, S 5–7m, often branching low down, with an untidy crown. Widespread in drier habitats, often forming thickets; a pioneer tree in disturbed ground. **Bark:** Dark brown to black, with deep, regular fissures. Young twigs grey-brown to reddish. Thorns are paired, long, slender, 4–9cm, typically pointing backwards. **Leaves:** Alternate, compound, bipinnate, with 2–11 pairs of pinnae clustered at spinal nodes, 7–25 opposite pairs of narrow leaflets, 7 x 1.5mm, grey-green. Petiole short. **Flowers:** Sep–Apr, in pairs at spine nodes,

stalked balls, < 2cm, bright yellow, fragrant; with the new leaves. **Fruit:** Mar–Sep, a long, straight or slightly curved, fattish, sweet-smelling indehiscent pod, 8–17cm, black, constricted between the seeds. Pod segments break off, splitting explosively to release 10–14 flat brown seeds. **Notes:** Browsed by wildlife. Edible gum used in confectionary, pods for ink; bark to treat coughs. Can be invasive, excluding other species. **Other species:** 27 in Zambia and 8 subspecies: now separated into 14 *Vachellia* species (pom-pom flowers) and 13 *Senegalia* species (flowers borne in spikes). *A. karroo* similar, but leaflets more spaced and angled.

BEST SEEN

North and South Luangwa, Lower Zambezi, Lochinvar and Kafue

Acacia robusta Splendid Acacia

(= *VACHELLIA ROBUSTA*) IN ZAMBIA SUBSP. *CLAVIGERA*: a tall, near-evergreen tree, H 20m, but usually shorter, S 8–20m, with a straight trunk, spreeding branches, and a distinctly flattish but spiky crown. Confined to the drier south at low altitudes in wooded grassland, riverine fringes and near water. **Bark:** Grey to dark brown, sometimes smooth, usually deeply vertically fissured. Thorns paired and straight at nodes. **Leaves:** Alternate, compound, bipinnate, with 2–6 pairs of pinnae, each with 10–25 opposite pairs of small leaflets, 8 x 2mm, spaced slightly apart, dark green and paler below. Petiole 1–2cm. **Flowers:** Aug–Oct, on stalks in axillary clusters along branches, small balls, < 2cm, white and fragrant. **Fruit:** Oct–Feb, a large, narrow, sickle-shaped pod, < 19cm, thickened but not woody, with grey to dark brown linear markings, splitting along both sides to release up to 15 flat, ellipsoidal, brown seeds. **Notes:** Leaves and fruit are browsed by wildlife. Bark and roots are used in traditional medicine to treat schistosomiasis, sexually-transmitted diseases and stomach ailments. A good bee tree. **Other species:** 27 in Zambia and 8 subspecies: now separated into 14 *Vachellia* species (pom-pom flowers) and 13 *Senegalia* species (flowers borne in spikes).

BEST SEEN
Lower Luangwa, southern Kafue and Lower Zambezi

Acacia seyal White-galled Acacia

LOCAL NAMES: Musenzenze, Munyele

(= *VACHELLIA SEYAL*) IN ZAMBIA VAR. *FISTULA*: a small to medium-sized deciduous tree, H 9m, S 3–7m, with a crooked trunk, spreading branches, and untidy umbrella crown. Lower branches often burn off in grass fires. Confined to the Kafue Flats floodplain on seasonally flooded, heavy, cracking clays. **Bark:** Smooth, white with reddish-powdery covering over greenish under-bark. Thorns paired, white, straight, long, often with a swollen base formed from unoccupied ant galls. **Leaves:** Alternate, compound, bipinnate, 6–15cm, with 2–4 pairs of opposite pinnae, each with 6–12 pairs of small, opposite, partly overlapping leaflets, 8 x 2mm. Petiole short.

Flowers: Jun–Sep, on 2–4cm-long stems in branched, axillary or terminal heads, small balls, < 1.5cm, bright yellow, fragrant. **Fruit:** Jun–Aug, in clusters, a curved pod, 7–22cm, greenish-brown, tapering at both ends, constricted between seeds, splitting to release 6–12 elliptical brown seeds. **Notes:** A dry-season forage. Well-adapted to flooding and severe grass fires, it can shed burnt bark and regenerate. Bark has molluscicide properties. Ant galls may be occupied by successive species of ant, protecting the tree. **Other species:** 27 in Zambia and 8 subspecies: now separated into 14 *Vachellia* species (pom-pom flowers) and 13 *Senegalia* species (flowers in spikes).

BEST SEEN
Blue Lagoon and Lochinvar, and surrounding Kafue floodplain

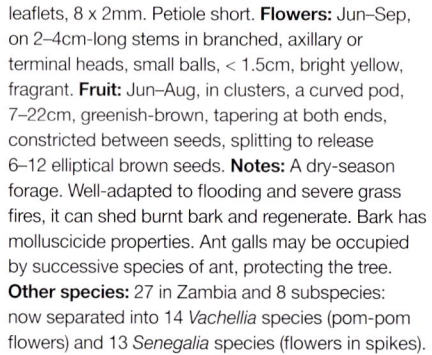

Acacia sieberiana **Paperbark Thorn**

(= *VACHELLIA SIEBERIANA*) IN ZAMBIA VAR. *WOODII*: a common, splendid deciduous tree, H 17m, S 10–15m, with a straight trunk, ascending branches and a flattened, wide canopy. Widespread except in the extreme northwest, usually in Munga woodland and wooded grassland on alluvial soils, occasionally in Mopane and Chipya woodland. **Bark:** Light grey, rough, peeling to reveal a yellowish under-bark. Young twigs covered in gold-yellow hairs. Thorns paired at nodes, straight, < 5cm. Older trees mostly thornless. **Leaves:** Alternate, compound, bipinnate, < 15cm, with 8–20 pairs of opposite pinnae, each with 15–45 opposite pairs of small oblong leaflets, 4 x 1mm, yellowish-green. Petiole 1cm. **Flowers:** Sep–Dec, in loose axillary heads, small balls, < 2cm, creamy-white and fragrant. **Fruit:** Mar onwards, an oblong semi-dehiscent pod, < 21cm, papery-pale brown, splitting long after falling to release 2–7 flat, elliptical, olive, grey-brown seeds. **Notes:** Pods favoured by wildlife, but hydrocyanic (prussic) acid is concentrated when leaves and pods are wilted. Bark and roots used as treatment for parasites, and to relieve bronchial and urinary tract infections. Gum used as ink. A bee tree. **Other species:** 27 in Zambia and 8 subspecies: now separated into 14 *Vachellia* species (pom-pom flowers) and 13 *Senegalia* species (flowers in spikes).

BEST SEEN
Most plateau and valley national parks, and Munga woodland

Acacia tortilis Umbrella Thorn

LOCAL NAMES: Mukoka, Mzunga, Nsangu, Nyoswa

(= *VACHELLIA TORTILIS*) IN ZAMBIA VAR. *SPIROCARPA*: a medium-sized semi-deciduous tree, H 20m, S 6–15m, with a straightish trunk, angled, spreading branches, and a characteristic flattish, dense umbrella crown and scrubby form. At low altitudes in northern, eastern, central and southern Zambia, usually in Kalahari, Munga and Mopane woodland. **Bark:** Dark brown to grey-black, deeply fissured, ridged. Younger branches grey-brown to salmon-pink and hairy. Thorns paired, variably long and slender, < 9cm, or short and hooked. **Leaves:** Alternate, compound, bipinnate, with 4–10 pairs of pinnae, each with 7–15 opposite pairs of very

small, narrow, overlapping leaflets, 5 x 1.5mm, bluish-green. **Flowers:** Nov–Jan, on loose axillary or terminal branched stalks, small round balls, < 3cm, white or creamy and fragrant. **Fruit:** Mar–Jun or later, in bunches, a narrow, twisted-contorted, dehiscent pod, 4–13cm, papery-pale brown, dropping and releasing 14 rounded, brown seeds, 5mm, with a horseshoe-shaped areole. **Notes:** Nutritious leaves and pods are heavily browsed by wildlife, and also an indicator of good grazing. Bark provides a good tannin. Tolerates drought and alkali soils. **Other species:** 27 in Zambia and 8 subspecies: now separated into 14 *Vachellia* species (pom-pom flowers) and 13 *Senegalia* species (flowers in spikes).

BEST SEEN
Nsumbu, North and South Luangwa, Lower Zambezi, Blue Lagoon and Lochinvar

Albizia adianthifolia Flat-crowned Albizia

A large, flat, crowned semi-deciduous tree, H 35m, S 6–15m, with a short trunk, branching upwards then spreading, and a light, feathery umbrella-shaped crown. Confined to the wetter north and east, usually in dry evergreen forest, and Miombo and Chipya woodland; common along northern roads. **Bark:** Dark brown, finely fissured with small squarish scales. Exudes a yellow gum when damaged. **Leaves:** Alternate, compound, bipinnate, with 4–8 pairs of pinnae, each with 5–17 pairs of opposite, rectangular leaflets, 2 x 0.7cm, dark green, with diagonal midrib. Under-leaf and petiole hairy. **Flowers:** Aug–Nov, in semicircular heads, 4–6cm, white petals with green stamens or pink tubes raised above the corolla. **Fruit:** May–Aug, a flat, oblong, dehiscent pod, 10–14cm, raised above the seeds, pale reddish-brown and finely hairy with conspicuous margin. Taking up to 9 months to mature. Distributed by wind, containing 5–12 round, dark brown seeds attached to the pod with a short filament. **Notes:** Wood produces a good finish. Leaves are browsed. The gum (reddish), roots and bark are used to treat skin diseases, inflamed eyes and bronchitis. A good plantation shade tree. **Other species:** 11 in Zambia: 3 are riverine/gallery forest species, 1 a small tree.

> **BEST SEEN**
> Northern plateau and national parks, and escarpment of South Luangwa

Albizia amara Bitter Albizia

LOCAL NAMES: **Mulalantete, Mukangala, Kasongu, Mkalanga, Kankumbwila**

IN ZAMBIA SUBSP. *SERICOCEPHALA*: a small to medium-sized semi-deciduous tree, H 18m, S 5–8m, resembling an *Acacia*, but thornless. Trunk often multi-stemmed, branches crooked, and crown flattish and open. Widespread in Chipya, Munga, Mopane and Kalahari woodland, often on termitaria and along dambos. **Bark:** Grey to dark brown, rough, deeply vertically fissured. Young branches with yellow hairs. Exudes a dark gum when damaged. **Leaves:** Alternate or opposite, compound, bipinnate, long, narrow, 15 x 3.5cm, with 15–35 pairs of pinnae, each with 40–50 pairs of small triangular leaflets, 4 x

1mm, greyish. Petiole 1–2cm. **Flowers:** Sep–Dec, in 'shaving brush'-like heads, 4–6cm across, white petals and pink stamens, fragrant. **Fruit:** Jun–Oct, a large pod, 10–20cm, papery-purplish with green margin, becoming brown, twisting, with 4–8 oval, dark brown seeds. **Notes:** Wood dark brown, gives a good finish. Leaves browsed by wildlife. Bark produces a poor-quality reddish gum, can be used as an adhesive. Roots and bark contain a saponin, used as soap. **Other species:** 11 in Zambia: 3 are riverine/gallery forest species, 1 a small tree. *A. harveyi* similar, but it has sickle-shaped leaflets.

BEST SEEN
Most woodland areas and national parks

Albizia antunesiana Purple-leaved Albizia

A medium-sized to large semi-evergreen tree, H 25m, S 6–10m, branching upward from a short trunk, with a light, umbrella-shaped crown. Occurs in most habitats except montane and swamp forest areas; common in Lake Basin Chipya and Kalahari woodland, often on termite mounds. **Bark:** Reddish, becoming dark grey-black, vertically fissured with raised scales. Exudes a crimson gum when damaged. **Leaves:** Opposite, compound, bipinnate, 13cm, with 2 or 3 pairs of pinnae, each with 5–9 pairs of opposite, oblique, large rhombic-ovate leaflets, 4 x 1.5cm, characteristically pale blue-green below and leaflet base asymmetric. Petiole short, 1–2cm.

Flowers: Aug–Oct, in large hemispherical, axillary or terminal bunched heads, < 5cm, fluffy and white, with stamens, < 3cm, fragrant. **Fruit:** May–Sep, a long, flat, oblong, pod, < 23cm, pale brown, raised at seed points, with 4–10 flat, yellow-green seeds. Remaining on the tree. **Notes:** A short-period bee tree. Roots contain a saponin, which can be used as soap. Sawdust from the wood is an irritant. **Other species:** 11 in Zambia: 3 are riverine/gallery forest species, 1 a small tree.

BEST SEEN
Most woodland areas and national parks

Albizia harveyi   Sickle-leaf Albizia

LOCAL NAMES: Mulalantanga, Mulalantete, Mukangala, Kalimika

A small to medium-sized *Acacia*-like deciduous tree, H 14m, S 5–8m, with a short and crooked trunk, branching upwards, and a rounded, open crown. Confined to the drier west, south and east, usually in Munga and Mopane woodland, typically on termite mounds and often gregarious. **Bark:** Variable, greyish-brown, deeply vertically fissured and ridged. Exudes a gum when damaged. **Leaves:** Alternate, compound, bipinnate, 13cm, with 18 pairs of pinnae, with 10–24 opposite pairs of small, narrow, pointed, sickle-shaped leaflets, 5 x 1.5mm, grey-green with midrib asymmetric. Petiole short and hairy.

Flowers: Sep–Nov, in semicircular axillary branched heads, small, white to yellowish and fragrant, with stamens, < 2cm. **Fruit:** Jun–Sep, a long, flat, oblong pod, 4–13cm, but < 25cm, papery-pale brown, rounded at both ends. Pods remain on the tree, slowly releasing 6–8 flat, brown seeds. **Notes:** Wood is heavy, strong and usable. Leaves and fruit are eaten by wildlife. Roots are used to treat swollen legs. **Other species:** 11 in Zambia: 3 are riverine/gallery forest species, 1 a small tree. Similar to *A. amara* but with distinctive sickle-shaped leaflets.

BEST SEEN
Eastern, southern and western national parks and woodland areas

Albizia tanganyicensis **Paper-bark Albizia**

A large, deciduous tree, H 20m, S 5–12m, with a straight or crooked trunk, branching upwards, and a rounded, open crown. Leafless for several months. Confined to the drier south and east at low to medium altitudes, usually in escarpment and rocky sites. Often near the other escarpment 'ghost tree' species: *Sterculia quinqueloba* and *S. africana*. **Bark:** Reddish outer bark sheds to show distinctive, smooth, whitish under-bark. **Leaves:** Opposite, compound, bipinnate, 6–14cm, with 3–7 pairs of pinnae, each with 5–13 pairs of large, asymmetrical obovate-elliptic leaflets, 3 x 0.9cm, light green. Petiole 2–5cm. **Flowers:** Aug–Oct, in semicircular axillary branched heads, greenish and fluffy, with creamy-white stamens, < 3cm. **Fruit:** Aug–Oct, a long, flat, oblong dehiscent pod, 10–35cm, pale glossy brown, releasing 6–8 flat, brown seeds. **Notes:** Sawdust from the wood is an irritant. Relatively easy to propagate, it makes a spectacular garden specimen tree. **Other species:** 11 in Zambia: 3 are riverine/gallery forest species, 1 a small tree.

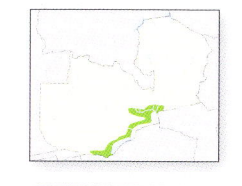

BEST SEEN
North and South Luangwa, and Lower Zambezi, and escarpments

Albizia versicolor Red Pod Albizia

LOCAL NAMES: Ifumangoma, Mubaba, Mupumangoma, Mpanga, Chisomwe

A medium-sized to large semi-deciduous tree, H 18m, S 8–12m, with a short, basally swollen trunk, upward-spreading branches, and a spreading, rounded, dense crown. Widespread, usually in Munga woodland, but found in all woodland types except montane forest. **Bark:** Variable, greyish-brown with wide, deep vertical fissures and rough scales. Exudes a sticky gum when damaged. **Leaves:** Opposite, compound, bipinnate, 6–14cm, with 2–6 opposite pairs of pinnae, with 5–13 pairs of large leaflets, 5.5 x 3cm, light green, densely hairy below, with midrib asymmetric. Petiole 2–5cm, with a conspicuous basal gland.

Flowers: Aug–Nov, in axillary bunched heads, semi-hemispherical, fluffy, white to yellowish, stamens pinkish, < 7cm, lasting only a few days. **Fruit:** Sep–Dec, a flat, oblong pod, < 27cm, crimson becoming red-brown, rounded at both ends, brittle, containing 6–8 flat, brown seeds. **Notes:** Sawdust is an irritant. New pods are poisonous, but eaten by wildlife when mature. Roots contain a saponin; burning roots used traditionally to treat mental health disorders. **Other species:** 11 in Zambia: 3 are gallery forest species.

BEST SEEN
Widespread, most plateau and valley national parks

Amblygonocarpus andongensis Scotsman's Rattle

A large deciduous tree, H 25m, S 8–18m, with a short trunk, upward-spreading branches, and a rounded feathery crown. Widespread but occasional at low and medium altitudes, usually on sandy soils in Kalahari and Munga woodland, but found in all woodland types. **Bark:** Light brown, becoming dark brown with vertical, weaving fissures and rough scales. **Leaves:** Alternate, compound, bipinnate, 15–30cm, with 2–5 pairs of subopposite pinnae, each with 5–9 pairs of large, subopposite, ovate leaflets, 3 x 2cm, blue-green. Petiole 4–9cm. **Flowers:** Sep–Nov, single or in pairs, in drooping axillary spikes, 6–18cm, creamy-yellow and fragrant.
Fruit: May–Aug, often remaining to Oct, a characteristic, long, square, woody pod, < 17cm, glossy red-brown, with a distinctly turpentine smell (12 per cent linoleic acid), with 6–10 brown seeds in a spongy matrix. **Notes:** Wood dark red, hard and strong. Fallen pods are quickly invaded by borers. Oil from the pods used as a fish poison. A good garden shade tree. **Other species:** This single-species genus is restricted to Africa.

> ### BEST SEEN
> Most plateau and valley national parks with medium-altitude Munga woodland

Dichrostachys cinerea Sickle Bush

LOCAL NAMES: Kansalosalo, Katenge, Kaweyi, Muselesele

An untidy, spiny semi-deciduous shrub or small tree, H 10m, S 4–8m, usually multi-stemmed, with a feathery crown. Forms thickets by suckering on abandoned farmland. Occurs widely at lower altitudes in most woodland types, *Baikiaea* forest and abandoned farmland. **Bark:** Grey-black, fissured, with weaving vertical ridges. Spines straight and grey. **Leaves:** Alternate, compound, bipinnate, 8–20cm, with 6–19 pairs of pinnae, each with 8–40 opposite pairs of small, narrow, oblong, sickle-shaped leaflets, 10 x 3mm, dark green, closing up at midday. Petiole 2cm. **Flowers:** Aug–Dec, often later,

in axillary spikes, 2–5cm, hanging upside-down, with a pink sterile spike above a short, bright yellow fertile catkin. **Fruit:** May–Sep, often remaining on the tree, a clustered, black-brown twisted pod, < 10cm, constricted between seeds, with 4–6 flat, glossy brown seeds. **Notes:** Wood makes a quality charcoal. Inner bark makes a good string. Leaves and pods are good browse, high in protein and minerals. Roots are used for baskets. Leaves and roots are used in traditional medicine to treat snakebite and burns. **Other species:** Numerous subspecies across Africa and Asia; 11 other species in the Old World tropics.

BEST SEEN
Unobtrusive, but in most valley-area national parks and in abandoned farmland

Entada abyssinica Tree Entada

A sprawling, deciduous shrub or small tree, H 10m, S 4–7m, with a short trunk, spreading branches, and a light, rounded crown. Occurs in most woodland types, usually at lower altitudes and frequently in Chipya and Mopane woodland, but not in the southwest. Sometimes invades disturbed land. **Bark:** Red-brown, smooth with corky spots, becoming grey-brown, rough, cracked and scaly. **Leaves:** Alternate, compound, bipinnate, 8–20cm, with 2–20 pairs of pinnae, each with 25–55 pairs of small, opposite, narrow, oblong leaflets, 8 x 2mm, light green, with midrib asymmetric. Petiole variable. **Flowers:** Nov–Dec, in fluffy axillary spikes, < 14cm, small, creamy-white to yellowish, fragrant. **Fruit:** Apr–Aug, a flat pod, 15–40cm, pale brown, with outer coat peeling off to reveal numerous papery segments, each with 1 flat, dark brown seed. Seed segments fall off individually, leaving a woody rim. **Notes:** Bark and roots contain a saponin and an alkaloid. Few medicinal uses. The tree features in rain-making ceremonies. **Other species:** 6 in Zambia and 2 subspecies: 1 is a climber similar to *E. abyssinica* and 1 is a **Vulnerable** suffrutex. Distinctive packet-like seeds separate this species from otherwise similar *Albizia* species.

BEST SEEN
All valley national parks except the southwest

Faidherbia albida Winter Thorn

A large deciduous tree, H 30m, S 30m, with a straight trunk, heavy, spreading branches, and a rounded crown. Leafless in the wet season. Widespread at low and medium altitudes, usually in riverine/alluvial situations; sometimes in extensive cohorts in Kalahari and Mopane woodland, but not in parts of the north and northwest. Occasionally in most other woodlands. **Bark:** Whitish to dark grey-brown, rough, cracked and scaly. Spines paired, straight, 2cm. **Leaves:** Alternate, compound, bipinnate, 8–20cm, with 3–10 pairs of pinnae, each with 6–20 opposite pairs of small, asymmetric-elliptic leaflets, 5 x 2mm, grey-green. Petiole 2–3.5cm. **Flowers:** May–Sep, in slender axillary spikes, < 14cm, creamy-white and fragrant. **Fruit:** Jul–Sep, a curled, twisted indehiscent pod, < 20cm, bright orange becoming pale brown, opening on the ground, with 10 glossy brown seeds in a spongy matrix. **Notes:** Pods, leaves and bark are browsed by elephant and other herbivores, but pods contain poisonous hydrocyanic (prussic) acid when young. The species indicates good soils. Used extensively in agroforestry, fixing nitrogen by bacterial symbiosis. **Other species:** A single species across Africa and the Eastern Mediterranean.

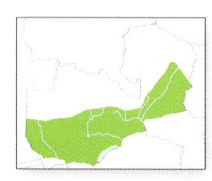

BEST SEEN
Common in all valley national parks and alluvial valleys

Parkia filicoidea Locust Bean

LOCAL NAMES: Musepa, Mkundi, Mpeza, Msenya

A large semi-deciduous tree, H 30m, S 30m, with a triangularly buttressed trunk, upward-spreading branches and a rounded crown. Relatively uncommon, confined to the wetter north, mainly in riverine and gallery forest. **Bark:** Whitish-brown to dark grey, smooth, with shallow, vertical furrows. Exudes a slimy orange resin when damaged. **Leaves:** Alternate, compound, bipinnate, 30cm, with 4–11 pairs of opposite or subopposite pinnae, each with 8–18 opposite pairs of large, asymmetric-oblong leaflets, 4 x 1.5cm, dark green, middle ones largest. Petiole short. **Flowers:** Aug–Nov, clustered in light-bulb-shaped flowerheads, 5–7cm in diameter at the end of 50cm-long stalks, hairy, pink-red, nectar-rich and with unpleasant smell. **Fruit:** Nov–Feb, in bunches of 3–5, a large, curved, indehiscent pod, 25–80cm, glossy brown and leathery, constricted between seed points. Pods fall releasing 20–30 flat, brown seeds in a pinkish, floury and sweet edible matrix. **Notes:** Flowers attract bats and squirrels. Pods are browsed by herbivores; pods and bark contain a viable tannin. A nitrogen-fixing plant. **Other species:** 2 other species in Africa, but this genus has a worldwide distribution.

BEST SEEN

Luapula Valley and national parks in eastern and northern Zambia

Acacia xanthophloea **Fever Tree**

(= *VACHELLIA XANTHOPHLOEA*) A medium-sized to large, spiny, semi-deciduous tree, H 25m, S 8–15m, often multi-branched, with a straight trunk, drooping branch ends, and an open, umbrella-shaped crown. Typical in low-lying, swampy alluvial valleys in East and southern Africa. Shares same habitat as malarial mosquito, hence it used to be associated, mistakenly, with malarial fevers. **Bark:** Yellow-green, smooth, sometimes flaking. Photosynthesis occurs in the bark. Spines paired at nodes, straight, < 7cm, white. **Leaves:** Bipinnate, with 4–7 pairs of opposite pinnae, each with 10–17 pairs of fine leaflets, 8 x 2mm. Petiole short. **Flowers:** Sep–Nov, on short stalks, clustered at nodes and branch ends, yellow-cream balls, < 2cm, fragrant. **Fruit:** Jan onwards, a flat, oblong, papery pod, < 19cm, constricted between seeds, red to pale brown. Segments break to release 5–10 elliptical green seeds. **Notes:** Not naturally occurring in Zambia. Timber usable. Bark used to treat sickle cell anaemia and indigestion. Germinates easily and grows fast. **Other species:** 27 in Zambia and 8 subspecies: now separated into 14 *Vachellia* species (pom-pom flowers) and 13 *Senegalia* species (flowers in spikes).

Delonix regia **Flamboyant**

A medium-sized deciduous tree, H 12m, S 8–12m, with a short trunk and heavy lateral branches. **Bark:** Grey-brown, becoming cracked and scaly. **Leaves:** Bipinnate, < 60cm, with 15–25 pairs of feathery pinnae, each with 20–30 pairs of oblong leaflets, bright green. Leafless in the dry season. **Flowers:** Oct–Dec, abundant and distinctive, in clumps at branch ends, < 8cm, with 4 reddish-orange to scarlet petals, and a fifth, larger, upright yellow-and-white-spotted standard petal. **Fruit:** Apr–Jun, a long, flattened, pea-like pod, < 60cm, green and leathery, becoming dark brown, splitting to release numerous yellowish seeds. **Notes:** Introduced from Madagascar's dry deciduous forests (where it is now endangered) to Mauritius in the 1820s, then distributed across the tropics. Widely planted, also grown as a bonsai specimen. Heavy lateral branches often break off suddenly. Few plant species grow well under Flamboyants. **Other species:** 11 in tropical Africa, Madagascar and India.

Jacaranda mimosifolia Jacaranda

A deciduous or semi-evergreen tree, H < 25m, S 4–10m, sometimes multi-stemmed, with drooping branches and a spreading crown. **Bark:** Pale grey and smooth, becoming cracked and scaly. **Leaves:** Compound, bipinnate, < 45cm, with 15–20 pairs of pinnae, each with 14–30 pairs of pointed leaflets, 1.5 x 0.4cm, grey-green. **Flowers:** Aug–Sep, bunches of blue-violet 'bells', < 8cm; many trees flower simultaneously before the new leaves. **Fruit:** Oct–Dec, a flattened, round, splitting pod 5cm, brown, wooden, releasing many winged seeds. **Notes:** An introduced species, now invasive, native to northern Argentina and southern Bolivia, where it is now threatened. Widely planted for shade and the spectacular spring flowering. The

wood is pale and soft; it turns well to make bowls. Bees favour the nectar. Few plant species grow well under Jacarandas. **Other species:** 29 species in tropical South America. **Legislated as invasive in South Africa and parts of Australia.**

Spathodea campanulata African Tulip Tree

A medium-sized semi-evergreen tree, H 25m, S 8–12m, sometimes multi-stemmed, with a dense, closed crown. **Bark:** Dark brown, rough, deeply cracked and scaly. **Leaves:** Compound, imparipinnate, < 30cm, with 9–15 pairs of leaflets, 9 x 3cm, dark green, leathery, hairy below. **Flowers:** Nov–Jan, showy in clumps on branch ends, trumpet-shaped, 8–15cm, reddish-orange. **Fruit:** Jan onwards, a large, dark brown, cigar-shaped pod, 15–20cm, splitting into 2 boat-shaped halves, releasing numerous white-winged seeds. **Notes:** Introduced from tropical West and Central Africa. Widely planted. Wood is pale and soft, used for drums and bellows. Bark and leaves have laxative and antibiotic properties, also anti-malaria action. Boiled seeds are used for arrow poison. Regarded as invasive in several countries. **Other species:** A single-species genus in Africa.

Bibliography

Astle, W.L., Phiri, P.S.M. & Prince, S.D. 1997. A Dictionary of Vernacular-Scientific Names of Plants of the Mid-Luangwa Valley, Zambia. *Kirkia* 16(2): 161–203. National Herbarium & Botanic Gardens, Harare.

Burrows, J. & Burrows, S. 2003. *Figs of Southern and South-Central Africa*. Umdaus Press, Hatfield.

Carr, N. 1977. *Some Common Trees and Shrubs of the Luangwa Valley*. Wildlife Conservation Society of Zambia, Ndola.

Centre for International Forestry Research (CIFOR). 2014. Zambia Country Profile: Monitoring, Reporting and Verification for REDD+. *Occasional Paper* 113. Bogor Barat, Indonesia.

Coates Palgrave, M. 2005. *Keith Coates Palgrave Trees of Southern Africa*. Struik Publishers, Cape Town.

Fanshawe, D.B. 1971. The Vegetation of Zambia. *Forest Research Bulletin* 7. Division of Forest Research, Kitwe.

Fanshawe, D.B. 1972. *Useful Trees of Zambia for the Agriculturalist*. Ministry of Land and Natural Resources, Lusaka.

Fanshawe, D.B. 1973. Check List of the Woody Plants of Zambia Showing Their Distribution. *Forest Research Bulletin* 22. Ministry of Land and Natural Resources, Lusaka.

Flora Zambesiaca, Royal Botanic Gardens, Kew. The *Flora* is a set of volumes, each edited by specific individuals, covering all the plant families in the FZ area. Some volumes are in several series. The *Flora* was freely used during the compilation of this publication.

Phiri, P.S.M. 2005. A Checklist of Zambian Vascular Plants. *SABONET* Report 32. Southern African Botanical Diversity Network, Pretoria.

Smith, P.P. & Allen, Q. 1995. *Common Trees, Shrubs and Grasses of the Luangwa Valley*. Trendrine Press, St Ives.

Smith, P.P. & Allen, Q. 2004. *Field Guide to the Trees and Shrubs of the Miombo Woodlands*. Royal Botanic Gardens, Kew.

Storrs, A.E.G. 1995. *Know Your Trees: Some Common Trees Found in Zambia*. Regional Soil Conservation Unit (RSCU), Nairobi.

Timberlake, J., Fagg, C. & Barnes, R. 1999. *Field Guide to the Acacias of Zimbabwe*. CBC Publishing, Harare.

Van Wyk, B. & Van Wyk, P. 2019. *How to Identify Trees in Southern Africa*. Struik Nature, Cape Town.

Vollesen, K. & Merrett, L. 2020. *A Field Guide to the (Wetter) Zambian Miombo Woodland: Part 1 (Ferns & Monocots), Part 2 (Dicots)*. GVPedia Communications.

Useful websites

African Plants: A Photo Guide **africanplants. senckenberg.de**

Flora of Zambia **zambiaflora.com**

Global Plants, JSTOR/ITHACA. **plants.jstor.org**

International Plant Names Index (IPNI) **ipni.org**

Luangwa Trees **mobile.sites.google.com/site/ luangwatrees/home**

Plants of the World Online **powo.science. kew.org**

South African National Biodiversity Institute **pza.sanbi.org**

ACKNOWLEDGEMENTS

This book would not have been possible without the input of many people. We would especially like to thank Alison Bingham Young (for accessing Mike Bingham's photographic archive), Bart Wursten (for providing photographs of difficult-to-access or poorly known plants), and Quentin Allen (for photographs, enthusiasm and patience). Braam van Wyk, John Burrows and Joan Young searched their archives and supplied photographs at short notice. Paul Smith kindly reviewed early draft material, Braam van Wyk provided an invaluable cross-check of photographs, and Emsie du Plessis cast a critical proofreader's eye over the proofs. Fil Hyde and Nick Wightman provided useful comments. Many guides and friends have put up with us for hours as we collected photographs of trees – they know who they are and we thank them for their long-suffering indulgence and support.

We thank Pippa Parker, Roelien Theron, Natalie Bell, Gillian Black and the Struik Nature team at Penguin Random House South Africa for their patience, essential guidance, advice and support as this book was put together.

Photographic credits

b = bottom, bl = bottom left, br = bottom right, l = left, m = middle, ml = middle left,
mr = middle right, r = right, t = top, tl = top left, tr = top right

AP = Adam Pope, BD = Bernard DUPONT from FRANCE, BL = Brett Lee, BvW = Braam van Wyk, BW = Bart Wursten, CB = Clare Barkworth, ES = Ed Sayer, GB = Guida Bellcross, GM = Godfridah Mbaulu, JB = John Burrows, JP = Jenica Pizzaro, JV = Jacy Vlachos, JY = Joan Young, MB = Mike Bingham, NW = Nick Wightman, PF = Peter Frost, QA = Quentin Allen, RP = Robin Pope, SA = stock.adobe.com, SB = African Plants – A Photo Guide. www.africanplants.senckenberg.de (continuously updated), SS = Sam Susu, WC = Wikimedia Commons

Front cover: JP
Back cover: t to b 1: CB, 2: MB, 3: QA, 4: CB, 5: BW
Title page: © ClaraNila, SA
Contents page: CB
4: © Pascal, SA
5 ml: CB, mr: © Samantha, SA, br: © Juan Carlos Munoz, SA
6: © Chipo, SA
7 t to b 1: AP, 2: Christine Coppinger, 3: CB, 4: Craig Zytkow
8 t to b 1: CB, 2: AP, 3: CB, 4: AP
9 t: AP, m and b: CB
10 all: AP
14: CB
15: CB
18 ml: CB, mr: MB, bl: MB, br: CB
19 bl: CB, mr: BW, br: CB
20 all: CB
21 ml: CB, mr: MB, bl: CB, br: CB
22 all: CB
23 all: CB
24 ml: SAplants, CC BY-SA 4.0, WC, mr: SAplants, CC BY-SA 4.0, WC, bl to r 1: JY, 2: Udo Reinhardt, CC BY-SA 4.0, WC, 3: JY
25 bl: BW, mr: BW, br: BW
26 ml: BW, mr: BD, CC BY-SA 2.0, bl: CB, br: BW
27 ml: QA, mr: SAplants, CC BY-SA 4.0, WC, bl: JY, br: CB
28 ml, mr and bl: CB, br: QA
29 all: CB
30 all: CB
31 bl: BvW, mr and br: CB
32 ml: CB, mr: BD, CC BY-SA 2.0, WC, bl and br: CB
33 bl: CB, mr: JY, br: brewbooks from near Seattle, USA, CC BY-SA 2.0, WC

34 ml and mr: GM, bl: AP, br: GM
35 ml, mr and bl: CB, br: SS
36 all: CB
37 bl and mr: CB, br: GB
38 ml: CB, mr: JB, bl and br: CB
39 ml and mr: CB, bl to r 1 and 2: CB, 3: QA
40 ml: BvW, mr: CB, bl: JMK, CC BY-SA 3.0, WC, br: CB
41 ml: Piet Grobler, CC BY-SA 3.0, WC, mr: QA, bl to r 1 and 2: CB, 3: JY
42 all: CB
43 all: CB
44 ml: QA, bl and br: CB
45 ml: BvW, mr: BW, bl and br: CB
46 all: CB
47 ml: SS, mr, bl and br: CB
48 ml: CB, mr: JB, bl: BW, br: CB
49 bl and mr: CB, br: QA
50 ml: QA, bl: CB, br: GB
51 bl: BvW, mr: BW, br: BW
52 all: CB
53 bl: MB, mr and br: BW
54 all: BW
55 ml: JP, mr: BW, bl: CB, br: BW
56: ml: JB, mr: © Günther Baumann, SB (2009), bl and br: JB
57 bl: JB, mr: NW, br: CB
58 tl and ml: MB, bl and br: JB
59 all: CB
60 ml: JB, mr and bl: Sue Christian Bell, CC BY-SA 3.0, WC, br: BW
61 ml: CB, mr: BvW, bl and br: CB
62 all: CB
63 bl: AP, mr: MB, br: AP
64 tl: CB, ml and bl: QA, br: CB
65 bl and mr: CB, br: QA

66 ml: QA, bl and br: JB
67 ml: JB, bl: JMK, CC BY-SA 3.0, WC, tr: GB, mr: JB, br: JY
68 all: CB
69 bl: CB, tr: SAplants, CC BY-SA 4.0, WC, mr and br: CB
70 all: CB
71 bl: CB, tr: SS, mr: CB, br: CB
72 tl: SS, ml and mr: CB, bl: SAplants, CC BY-SA 4.0, WC, br: CB
73 bl: RP, mr: QA, br: CB
74 all: CB
75 ml: © Günther Baumann, SB (2007), mr: BvW, b: QA
76 all: CB
77 ml: CB, mr: RP, bl and br: CB
78 ml: CB, bl: Steven Haw, CC BY 2.0, WC, br: CB
79 bl: CB, mr and br: BW
80 all: CB
81 bl: SAplants, CC BY-SA 4.0, WC, mr: Rotational, Public domain, WC, br: BvW
82 tl: QA, ml, bl and br: GB
83 all: BW
84 ml: Manie Maree, CC BY-SA 4.0, WC, mr: CB, bl: AP, br: BvW
85 bl: CB, mr: Rotational, Public domain, WC, br: CB
86 all: CB
87 all: CB
88 ml: JV, bl: SS, br: AP
89 bl: CB, mr: JY, br: BW
90 ml: SAplants, CC BY-SA 4.0, WC, mr: JB, bl: MB, br: JY
91 ml: CB, mr: RP, bl to r 1: CB, 2: RP, 3: CB
92 ml and bl: CB, br: JB
93 bl: CB, tr: SS, mr and br: CB
94 ml: BvW, mr, bl and br: CB

Index

Scientific names are in italics. Alternative scientific names (synonyms) are redirected to accepted names currently in use in Zambia.

Young Luangwa hippos feeding beside mixed riverine trees